FRANCIS SCHAEFFER
THE MAN AND HIS MESSAGE

IN HONOR OF
THE 30TH ANNIVERSARY OF L'ABRI FELLOWSHIP
JUNE 5, 1955 – JUNE 5, 1985

LOUIS GIFFORD PARKHURST, JR.

TYNDALE HOUSE PUBLISHERS, INC.
WHEATON, ILLINOIS

All quotations from the book *The Tapestry* by Edith Schaeffer (Waco: Word Books, 1981) are used by permission of the publisher.

Unless otherwise noted, Scripture quotations in this book are taken from the *Holy Bible: New International Version.* Copyright © 1973, 1978 by the International Bible Society. Used by permission of Zondervan Bible Publishers.

Front cover illustration by John Robinette

First printing, October 1985

Library of Congress Catalog Card Number 85-51059
ISBN 0-8423-0923-3, paper 0-8423-0932-2, cloth

Printed in the United States of America

Dedicated to
the God who is there
Father, Son, and Holy Spirit
and to
L'Abri and the larger L'Abri family
past, present, and future

Those who are wise will shine
like the brightness of the heavens,
and those who lead many to righteousness,
like the stars for ever and ever.
Daniel 12:3

CONTENTS

APPENDIX

ACKNOWLEDGMENTS

THIS BOOK about Francis Schaeffer could not have been written apart from Edith Schaeffer's two books on their lives, *L'Abri* and *The Tapestry,* or apart from her personal ministry to me and to my family over the years I have known her. The biographical sketch on Francis Schaeffer "The Man," is based upon the books by Edith Schaeffer, upon many visits with members of the Schaeffer family, upon visits with members, workers, and students at L'Abri, and upon visits with people who have known their work for many years, but who have not been directly a part of it.

I have had the opportunity to be at L'Abri branches in Gryon and Huémoz, Switzerland, and in Rochester, Minnesota, U.S.A. These branches of L'Abri carry on extremely helpful and competent ministries. As I began work on this book, I was surprised to recollect how many members and workers of L'Abri I have met, visited with, and heard speak personally from every branch of L'Abri. I would like especially to thank Rochester L'Abri workers Ann Brown, Julie Cooper, Diane Gothrup, Greg and Mary Jane Grooms, and Jim and Gail Ingram for their friendship and ministry.

In a very special way, however, this book is based upon my knowledge of Dr. Francis Schaeffer through our personal relationship. I met him six years ago in Rochester, Minnesota, while he was undergoing treatment for cancer through the Mayo Clinic. I listened to his tapes, read his books, viewed his films, and attended his seminars and Monday night discussions. We marched together, six of us, to protest the abortions being performed in Rochester. We celebrated his last communion together, at his hospital bed, a few months before he died. I saw him at some of his triumphs, as well as at some of his lowest points at home and in the hospital.

I initially visited with him to learn about historic biblical Christianity, and as a result, I became a Bible-believing Christian and a more faithful pastor. We prayed together about various problems. His ministry to me was always helpful and practical, as I, like every other Christian, have had many battles to fight since becoming a Christian. I told him on several occasions: "I am a Bible-believing Christian today because of you—because you got cancer and came to Rochester. That is not to say that God gave you cancer so that I could become a Christian, but it is to say that in the midst of fighting your cancer you still reached out to me to help me become a Christian and a better minister." Many others have had the same life-changing experience from knowing him.

The format for the second part of the book, "His Message," was suggested to me by two people. First, Ranald Macaulay, one of Dr. Schaeffer's sons-in-law and now President and International Director of L'Abri (Dr. Schaeffer's successor), suggested that I emphasize Dr. Schaeffer's biblical foundation clearly, because this is an area that so many reviewers had overlooked as they had focused upon his intellectual innovations or his philosophical theology. Second, Debby Middelmann, Dr. Schaeffer's youngest daughter and co-director of Swiss L'Abri in Gryon, suggested that I use as an outline Dr. Schaeffer's book *Basic Bible Studies,* especially to give me reasonable boundaries as I introduce people to her father's massive works of books, tapes, and films. I was pleased with both of these suggestions, first, because I agree with Ranald's assessment, and second, Debby's is so practical. Except in the first three chapters and in the last chapter, where I expound his thought, I try to follow the general sequence of *Basic Bible Studies.* The first three chapters show why biblical Christianity is so crucial and the last chapter tells how to become a Christian.

Since this book is in honor of thirty years of L'Abri, the final section includes current listings of L'Abri books, tapes, and films so that any of these materials can be purchased directly from L'Abri Cassettes, or otherwise rented or purchased from others. I wish to thank Richard W. Cook of Sound Word Associates for kindly providing the bibliography included here, under the title "The Works of L'Abri." The chapter "What Can We Learn from Francis Schaeffer?" was kindly provided by my friend Larry Wilson, who was a pastor in Rochester and friend of Dr. Schaeffer during a portion of the time Dr. Schaeffer was being treated for cancer at the Mayo Clinic. Special thanks also to Mrs. Mary Louise Sather and Mrs. Virginia Muir for their careful editing and attention to factual detail on the manuscript of this book. However, any unintentional errors are the author's alone.

Besides acknowledging the cooperation of the Schaeffers and many others in L'Abri, too many to name and be fair to each one (except to mention that Edith Schaeffer and her personal secretary, Julie Cooper, aided me in some factual clarifications of the biographical sketch), I would like to thank my church for the sabbatical that made my trip to Switzerland possible, and for the personal advice of one of the members of my church, Jack Key, also the librarian of the Mayo Clinic.

One of the other joys that made this work possible was that my parents, Gifford and Trudie Parkhurst, and my wife's parents, Fred and Maxine Kirkham, could all come from Oklahoma at two different times to care for our children while my wife and I were in Switzerland. Finally, I must thank my wife, Pat, and my two children, Jonathan and Kathryn, for their understanding during the long hours I had to be away from them in the process of writing. My wife's advice and her loving support of the whole family was invaluable in the course of this project.

INTRODUCTION

FRANCIS AND EDITH SCHAEFFER began L'Abri Fellowship (*L'Abri* is French for "the shelter") in Switzerland in 1955. They desired to demonstrate by their words and work the existence of the God who is there.

Together, the Schaeffers achieved their purpose in many varied and surprising ways. Francis Schaeffer always spoke of his work in conjunction with his wife's: "You must read her books along with mine to see the balance of the total work we have tried to do with L'Abri over the years." He emphasized that he was not perfect, that their work was not perfect, that there was no perfection in L'Abri, but "if the choice in our lives is always between perfection and nothing, then we will always have nothing."

On the other hand, he believed that their work, along with all of the work of L'Abri, had been "substantial." He taught that Christians should be "substantially different" from what they were before they became Christians. He emphasized the importance of "substantial Christianity," and of continued growth toward Christian maturity in one of his most important books, *True Spirituality.*

The books of Francis and Edith Schaeffer go together. Edith Schaeffer really provided the foundation for them to have a Christian family, and she applied Christian faith practically to every part of their home life, including the raising of their children. Her many books cover areas of Christian family concern and tell of ways to develop what she calls "common-sense Christian living."

Francis Schaeffer, too, was concerned about the family, especially about the families of pastors, missionaries, and other Christian workers. He would sometimes seek out and talk to leaders of mission groups if he felt their evangelism methods were being destructive to the Christian families in their organization. Over the years of L'Abri, hundreds of young people from pastors' and missionaries' families have come to L'Abri, saying their parents' endeavors had destroyed their family life and this had turned them away from Christianity. Dr. Schaeffer said, "They came to L'Abri saying, 'You are our last hope!' " For hundreds, L'Abri was the first true family they had ever experienced, and those close to L'Abri feel a part of the "larger L'Abri family" or a vital part of the "praying family." Those who have gone to L'Abri, who became Christians there or who were Christians before they went, have sensed the reality of what it means to be a member of "God's family" now.

Edith's two books that tell the most about their lives, *L'Abri* and *The Tapestry,* total almost nine hundred pages. Both books must be read to understand more about their lives and work than I can highlight in this brief synopsis. The Schaeffers have written more than thirty books, made several films, and recorded hundreds of tapes. My book is only a "door to understanding" the richness of God's blessing in their lives and in L'Abri, and the scope of their teachings.

The first portion of this book, "The Man," is a brief biographical sketch of Francis Schaeffer. You will discover the reality of the God who is there in his life. His teachings should not be studied apart from trying to understand how he lived his teachings, especially in the work of L'Abri. In reading about his life in this book, you will discover the goals he set for himself and the type of Christian he tried to be. He tried to live consistently with what he taught so that his life would commend his faith.

But Francis Schaeffer would warn us not to become Christians simply because of someone else's life. If we do, our Christian faith will be based upon the imperfect example of a human being. Dr. Schaeffer was not perfect, and he never claimed to be. He made mistakes, as all of us do. Our faith must be based upon the objective truth of God's Word to us, the Bible. Dedicated lives in themselves are not a full demonstration of the God who is there. We must rely upon God's perfect Word, where there is no error, and where God has protected the authors from making any mistakes in their writing. There has been only one perfect human life on this earth, from birth to death, and that is the life of Jesus Christ, God's Son. Dr. Schaeffer's words and works always pointed people to that perfect one, who came to this earth, died, and rose again to be our Savior.

When we describe a Christian's life and work, we tend to focus only on the positive. While stressing the positive, we must also emphasize that all Christians have temptations, trials, and sorrows along the way. L'Abri was never an easy work, and it is less so today. As the Schaeffers fought on the Lord's side, Satan would often attack them fiercely. Edith's book *Affliction* is one of the best on that subject, because she wrote from personal experience. She finished it just one year before Francis Schaeffer learned he had cancer. Many people have read the book in times of trial. Pastors and other Christians in ministry have found that the book has given them something substantial to say as they have tried to help people who are suffering.

My purpose in writing this book on Francis Schaeffer is to show that there really is a God who is there. There is a God, not just in word or name only, but one who is really there. God makes a difference in our lives and in all of history. There is a God who is there, and he wants us to make a mark for him in history, not in our own strength or in our own way, but in his strength and in his way.

What we do in this life causes ripples throughout all history and for all eternity. Our ripples can be good and for God's Kingdom or they can be evil and for Satan's cause. We have a choice about what kind of ripples we are going to make in this life. We have a choice about what kind of God we are going to worship and obey. Edith has emphasized, "We are not chessmen being moved about by God. It is part of who we are. Our choices affect our own history and other people's history. We need to pray for each other with fervency that we are helped in our choices by the Lord, and not hindered by Satan's vile schemes."[1] We are ultimately going to serve the God who is there or fight against him and his purposes. It is our choice to make, and our choice will make an eternal difference. The choice we make should be made for good and sufficient reasons.

Many people need to see how the God who is there can make a difference in the lives of people who are dedicated to serving him and making him known. For some, the proof of the existence of God is in the substantial difference he makes in the lives of his followers. The Bible says our lives should demonstrate that we are Christians.

The second part of this book, "The Message," expounds in a simplified way Francis Schaeffer's teaching about the God who is there and what that must mean in the totality of our lives. He subtitled his complete works *A Christian Worldview,* because he wanted Christians to understand the Christian faith and the world as a whole rather than in fragments. Schaeffer taught that if we are really to understand who God is and what the Bible teaches, we must also understand what God is not and what the Bible does not teach. I follow that method in my presentation of his thought.

Many people who call themselves Christians believe and act out their faith in a fragmented way, because they do not understand that Christianity is systematic, reasonable, and applicable to all of life. The fourteen chapters in "The Message" teach not only what Francis Schaeffer taught, in a simplified form, but they show the foundation for a systematic biblical Christianity *in faith and life.*

I have used Dr. Schaeffer's *Basic Bible Studies* in my church with people who needed to know about Christianity prior to becoming Christians and members of my church, and I have also used it with groups of people who have been church members for a long time, but have wanted to know the Bible better as a whole. With both groups, the book has been an excellent resource. At the same time, I found that I was better able to teach the class and answer the questions that came up for discussion because I had read all of Dr. Schaeffer's books, seen all of his films, heard him answer countless questions, and also had the opportunity of asking him questions that troubled me. This background and perspective is not readily available to everyone who would like to use, or should use, *Basic Bible Studies*. And so I believe that by following the format Debby Middelmann suggested, my book could be used as a companion study guide for anyone wanting to teach or use *Basic Bible Studies*.

In studying the thought of Francis A. Schaeffer, it is important for us to realize that he was first of all biblical. When we understand the Bible as a systematic whole, from Genesis to Revelation, then we are able to relate the Christian faith to our lives in a more helpful and practical way. Our methods of evangelism also become more helpful and practical as we relate Scripture's truths to people in ways that hold together from beginning to end, instead of just giving them "truths that hang in the air."

Dr. Schaeffer read deeply and daily in the Bible. He strived to walk each day in prayerful practice of what the Bible taught. For these reasons, God gave him great insight into the Bible's teachings and how they relate to modern life. This does not mean that Dr. Schaeffer's thoughts about the Bible and its answers to the problems of modern man came easily to him. He sometimes spent several years thinking through to the Bible's answer to a particular question. The answers he gave appeared to be effortless, and they were often repeated, but this was so because he had spent many days of prayer and humble seeking for the answers in the Word of God. He tried to be very careful and precise when he gave his answers the best way that he could under the Lord's leading.

The Bible's answers that Dr. Schaeffer gave to questioning modern man were sometimes expressed in words that are difficult to understand. However, he found that his particular use of language really communicated to those who were asking the questions. Many of his questioners had steeped themselves in modern philosophical and theological thought, ending in despair; they had come out believing that everything was meaningless, even their own lives.

One young man, who is a missionary now, told me: "When I read his *Escape from Reason* in 1969, I found Dr. Schaeffer discussing every single writer that I had read. I was really messed up. I had been on drugs, in and out of mental hospitals. My parents had given up on me, and as far as I was concerned everything was blackness! Now, in 1984, I see young college students acting out and living the same blackness that I had lived in; they just don't know the name for it or the cause of it. I knew the hopelessness of modern philosophical thought from my deep study of the different writers that Dr. Schaeffer discussed in his books." Dr. Schaeffer's application of the Bible's answers in his special terminology reached some people who had been untouched by other language. And he was right when he said, "I think that my books are more contemporary now than when they were written."

In "The Message," I avoid as much as possible the use of Dr. Schaeffers' *special* language, and also most philosophical and theological academic terms. I do so for two reasons. One, I want to communicate the truths Dr. Schaeffer discovered in the Bible to people, both inside and outside the church, whose ways of thinking I know. I don't want to be "too technical." I hope this book will encourage some of them to read Dr. Schaeffer's books. I want to give people a greater ability to understand his thoughts and increase their confidence in their ability to comprehend new ways of speaking, writing, and thinking. Two, I believe many people with philosophical and theological backgrounds can read Dr. Schaeffer easily and critically (though with my own background in these areas I find that reading him several times is most helpful and avoids misunderstanding).

I hope my more simple presentation will help some to see his thought as a whole, and will help some to present the Christian faith more clearly and easily to the many who do not have training in sophisticated theological and philosophical areas. From over twelve years of pastoral ministry, I know that it is not easy to communicate complicated, but vitally important, Christian truths.

Since this is my goal, in this book I have refrained from getting into the name-calling, hairsplitting, and infighting that Dr. Schaeffer deplored among true Bible-believing Christians within some theological circles. I have chosen to emphasize the essentials of biblical truth in contrast to those in the churches who deny the essentials. This was Dr. Schaeffer's approach. At this point, I suggest that you read the article, "What Can We Learn from Francis Schaeffer?" by Larry Wilson in the Appendix of this book.

Dr. Schaeffer was sometimes accused of taking a mechanical approach to evangelism, but he consistently warned against this. If you are a Christian, do not try to use the Bible-based material in this book in a mechanical way to help others become Christians. You will not help very many become Christians simply by answering their questions, even with the right biblical answers, in an impersonal or "canned" manner. Dr. Schaeffer never approached anyone as if he were a machine or just a mind in a body. Dr. Schaeffer spoke to people from a loving and compassionate heart, to just that person and his problems—*personally.* He prayed for the person who was asking him questions, and he prayed while giving his answers. Others were involved in this praying too, as members of his family or of the larger L'Abri family were nearby, out of earshot of the conversation perhaps, but very much in prayer for Dr. Schaeffer and the person he was speaking to. Prayer was of vital importance, because Dr. Schaeffer knew that no one ever becomes a Christian apart from the active work of the Holy Spirit as the truth of God's Word is given. Satan does do all he can to blind the person seeking God's truth, and the habits of sin have so blinded and deafened others that only the Holy Spirit can conquer Satan or heal the eyes and ears for the hearing, receiving, and accepting the truth of God. In describing how a person becomes a Christian, Dr. Schaeffer said, "I know constantly that the grace of God is at work."

Francis Schaeffer has said that there is only one reason to be a Christian, and that is because Christianity is true. Our lives and our work should demonstrate that Christianity is true, but since our lives are so imperfect, we must direct people to the perfect God who is there and to his perfect Word, the Bible.

However, what does his perfect Word teach? To many the Bible is a closed book or a confusing book at best. Francis Schaeffer realized that the Bible teaches in a systematic and reasonable way the truth about the God who is there and his work in history. He taught that the Bible is true to reality, and this truth should make a difference in the way we live. Francis Schaeffer's work is beautiful, because he taught Christianity in a reasonable and systematic way so people could see that it was true and accept Christ as their Lord and Savior by grace through faith. He taught Christianity in a way that people could then reason about and reasonably share. He tried to live this way, and he wanted L'Abri to demonstrate the truth of the Bible in its work.

I hope some of the people who read this book will be able to say for the first time, "Oh, now I know about biblical Christianity, about the existence of the real God who is there, and about what that difference is going to make in existence. Now I know what it means to become a Bible-believing Christian, how to become a Bible-believing Christian, and what difference that should make in my life in practical ways. Now I have a faith I can really share with others in my words and in my life. I want to learn all I can about these ideas in further study, so I can help others find the God who is there and understand his truth. Oh, how I love God for who he is and for what he has done!"

I want to emphasize that this book is only a "door to understanding" Dr. Francis Schaeffer, his thought, and L'Abri. It cannot take the place of the many books and films created by Francis and Edith Schaeffer and others from L'Abri. What they have written needs to be read and read again, thought about and thought about again, lived and tried, and lived through again in a more substantial way. This is the only way to truly appreciate their work, and I believe that you will be a better servant of the Lord Jesus Christ if you make this effort. Also, I believe Dr. Schaeffer would want all of us to try to share his work with others in our own ways, and hopefully in better ways.

Some will want to have the opportunity of studying at L'Abri, of hearing the tapes, live lectures, and discussions. There are several branches of L'Abri. When Dr. Schaeffer died, the memorials sent in his name were given for the ongoing work of L'Abri, and not for a stone monument. L'Abri, and not the books and tapes, is his living memorial. The Appendix includes the address of each L'Abri branch.

Dr. Schaeffer's life was not an end in itself; no Christian's life should be. He thought, lived, and wrote so people everywhere could come to know God, glorify God, and also *enjoy* God and his works. This book has that goal in view. My prayer is that sometime before you close this book you will come to praise and thank God for what he has done, that you will come to know him truly, and that you will truly enjoy your relationship with the God who is there, through Jesus Christ our Lord and Savior.

L. G. Parkhurst, Jr.

1. *The L'Abri Family Letter,* July 17, 1984, page 5, by Edith Schaeffer. In the following pages, I have tried to footnote all written sources. Many of my quotations are from personal comments made to me by Dr. Schaeffer, or remarks he made in group meetings which I attended. I am not able to date these quotations as to time and place. Neither can I give credit here to each person who has told me each incident that I am reporting. Because of my personal and sometimes pastoral relationship with the Schaeffers, I have chosen to omit some names of people and places that would satisfy the curious but not change the substance of the evaluation.

FRANCIS A. SCHAEFFER IV

THE MAN

REMEMBER YOUR LEADERS, WHO SPOKE THE WORD OF GOD TO YOU. CONSIDER THE OUTCOME OF THEIR WAY OF LIFE AND IMITATE THEIR FAITH. JESUS CHRIST IS THE SAME YESTERDAY AND TODAY AND FOREVER. DO NOT BE CARRIED AWAY BY ALL KINDS OF STRANGE TEACHINGS. HEBREWS 13:7-9

1
FINDING THE TRUTH

FRANCIS AUGUST SCHAEFFER IV had a close and personal friendship with God. Shortly after he learned he had cancer, he said, "I know that my cancer has something to do with the battle in the heavenlies, and it makes a difference how I live, whether or not I will live according to what I profess and know to be true about historic Christianity." He fought cancer and other battles for five and half more years. The day before he died he prayed simply, "Dear Father God, I have finished my work. Please take me home. I am tired." God honored his request.

Before he died, Francis Schaeffer had become one of the most respected and influential Bible-believing Christians of the twentieth century. U.S. Surgeon General, Dr. C. Everett Koop, called him "God's man for this era." After Dr. Schaeffer's death, President Ronald Reagan wrote to his family, "He will long be remembered as one of the great Christian thinkers of our century."

Dr. Billy Graham said of him, "He was truly one of the great evangelical statesmen of our generation. He was no ivory-tower intellectual, but had a deep love for people and a profound commitment to evangelism. More than virtually any other thinker, he had keen insight into the major theological and philosophical battles of our time."[1] Another noted evangelical leader, Cal Thomas, summed up the Christian community's evaluation of Dr. Schaeffer when he wrote: "What more could be said of a life than this: that he glorified and magnified God, won men and women to Christ, and was faithful to the truth, the inerrancy, the infallibility of the Word of God to the end?"[2]

Dr. Schaeffer said of himself, "I really am a country preacher. But I have had to develop my philosophy to speak to a world that no longer believes that truth exists."[3]

Who was this man Schaeffer, and who made him what he was? How did he live out his message to those living in the second half of the twentieth century, and beyond? In the pages that follow you will be given a glimpse of this remarkable man.

Francis Schaeffer was a man of the Bible. He endeavored to live as a Christian balanced in two scriptural relationships, with God and the world. On the one hand, he endeavored to fulfill this admonition:

> Therefore, I urge you, brothers, in view of God's mercy, to offer your bodies as living sacrifices, holy and pleasing to God—which is your spiritual worship. Do not conform any longer to the pattern of this world, but be transformed by the renewing of your mind. Then you will be able to test and approve what God's will is—his good, pleasing, and perfect will.
>
> For by the grace given me I say to every one of you: Do not think of yourself more highly than you ought, but rather think of yourself with sober judgment, in accordance with the mea-

sure of faith God has given you . . . Love must be sincere. Hate what is evil; cling to what is good. Be devoted to one another in brotherly love. Honor one another above yourselves. Never be lacking in zeal, but keep your spiritual fervor, serving the Lord. Be joyful in hope, patient in affliction, faithful in prayer. Share with God's people who are in need. Practice hospitality. (Romans 12:1-3, 9-13)

Fulfilling Saint Paul's admonition, as Paul had revealed the will of God, did not come easily to Dr. Schaeffer. Christians are born supernaturally, but they must grow before they mature. Schaeffer did not become a Christian until he was seventeen, and later he went through a terrible time of doubt in Switzerland. It is not easy for anyone to live the Christian life, and Dr. Schaeffer always emphasized that neither he nor L'Abri was perfect. L'Abri was hard work. Still, as you read the following pages, you will find Dr. Schaeffer striving to attain these goals of God for his life.

The other words of Scripture describe what many people saw in Dr. Schaeffer. He was "a man of sorrows." Like the weeping prophet, Jeremiah, he cried for the condition of our world, and he cried for people individually. He saw and suffered from the effects of living in a fallen world, vastly unlike the world God created before man rebelled against him. He tried to rescue as many as he could from disobedience to God and the destructive results of sin. And at the same time, he spoke out against man's rebellion wherever he saw it, both in and outside the church. He often said, "We don't have the luxury of fighting the battle only on one front." He engaged in spiritual warfare; sometimes the battles were physical, but more often they were intellectual, battles of ideas. He fought for truth, and he was encouraged by these words of Scripture:

> But we have this treasure in jars of clay to show that this all-surpassing power is from God and not from us. We are hard pressed on every side, but not crushed; perplexed, but not in despair; persecuted, but not abandoned; struck down, but not destroyed. We always carry around in our body the death of Jesus, so that the life of Jesus may also be revealed in our body. For we who are alive are always being given over to death for Jesus' sake, so that his life may be revealed in our mortal body. (2 Corinthians 4:7-11)

Dr. Schaeffer was a true Christian before anything else. He was steadfast in his service to God and his fellowman. He did not seek a fight, but in preaching the truth he expected opposition. He gave a ready defense for the faith. He did not fear to bear his testimony in enemy territory. He was single-minded in his efforts to glorify the Lord Jesus Christ in his life and thought. After he became a Christian, he taught and demonstrated that Christianity was a special way of life based upon clear thinking and a friendship with God, through faith in Jesus Christ.

"Many of us saw in Francis Schaeffer a faith, a love, an intellectual honesty, a sacrificial commitment and a holiness that put him far ahead of us, but through his hard work and humility we could see what God can do in a man totally dedicated to him. He gave us hope," declared one minister. What Christ did in him was so convincing, in spite of his imperfections, that he could call the multitudes to Christ, and they came; they came gladly to follow him.

Francis was born of German-English ancestry on January 30, 1912, in the tiny bedroom of his parents' Pastoria Street home in Germantown, Pennsylvania. Fran's parents gave little thought to raising him in a Christian home. Later, when he did become a Christian, they certainly made it clear that they did not want any son of theirs to be a minister. The fourth to bear the family name, Fran was expected to follow in his father's footsteps.

His father, Frank Schaeffer, was born in 1876, and his mother, Bessie Williamson Schaeffer, in 1880. Though both of them had had some religious training while growing up, they were not Christians. They did not raise Fran in a home where the Christian faith made any real or practical difference. One can hardly think of a less promising beginning for Christian service.

Fran was an only child. His mother, after reflecting upon her own difficult childhood, had resolved to have only one child. But that one child was a strong, active, intelligent, and healthy boy.

At a very early age, Fran learned from his parents to strive for excellence, to be persistent, and to work hard. Since his parents were not intellectuals, but hard-working practical people, they taught and expected Fran to do an honest day's labor for an honest day's wage. They planned for him to get a degree in engineering and design (a practical subject!) and then to work with his hands at the side of his father. He was to join them in an unthinking, independent, cradle-to-grave type of life.

Neither he nor his parents knew the joy and dignity that only God can give to any calling in this life. They did not realize that their particular skills and talents were God-given. Raised in a blue-collar home, Fran never deprecated working in the trades or in any other honest industry. He insisted, "The call to the ministry is no higher a calling than any other." Each person is responsible before God to do his will in whatever vocation he is fulfilling.

Fran's school records show that he was highly intelligent, but he simply did not apply himself to his studies. He saw no reason to work hard in intellectual endeavors and did not do so until after he became a Christian; then he became a straight A student. His family took vacations together, but the father and son's main enjoyment of life came from working together in the trades, even remodeling their own home together, with Fran running the electrical wiring.

While attending Roosevelt Junior High School and then Germantown High School, he took classes in the vocational and technical areas. His parents expected him to study engineering at Drexel Institute after graduation. His preparation for the future, therefore, consisted in the study of mechanical drawing, woodworking, metalwork, electrical design, and construction. From his practical-minded and hardworking parents, he learned the satisfaction of a job well done no matter what he did.

There were no discussions of philosophical or theological questions in his home, and no concern for cultural things either. His parents knew nothing about such things. Fran did not have his interest in the arts and music stimulated until after he had reached junior high. In religious matters, he picked out a church to attend only because his Boy Scout troop was sponsored by the First Presbyterian Church. Though he planned to work primarily with his hands, he proved to be an able speaker. When he was only eleven, he won a speech contest that was sponsored by the Scouts. By the time he graduated from high school, he was prepared to lay flooring, build garages, lay brick, spread cement, and do plumbing.

At seventeen, Francis Schaeffer became a Christian.

He had begun teaching English to a Russian immigrant, and he needed to buy an English grammar. After purchasing the book he wanted, he went home and was surprised to unwrap an introduction to Greek philosophy. This book grabbed his interest and opened the door to intellectual pursuits.

His studies led him to discover the basic philosophical questions about life and its meaning. Seeking answers to the questions posed by life and the philosophers, he listened carefully to the preaching of his liberal pastor and found that he didn't teach much more than a liberal social ethic. He read more and more philosophy, but neither liberalism nor philosophy answered his questions.

Out of a desire to be honest, and thinking that because of his disbelief he ought to quit the church, he decided to read the Bible for himself and see if it had the answers he was seeking. He read the Bible as he would have read any other book of philosophy, religion, or history. From his reading of the books of Genesis through Revelation, he discovered the answers to his questions. In the course of about six months, he came to be a Christian.

At first he did not know of any others who believed as he did. He couldn't talk to his parents, and they would not have understood how he could have moved from not knowing whether there was a God or not (agnosticism), to reading Ovid, to reading the Bible, and then to finding the answers he sought in the Word of God. Looking back upon that time he observed, "What rang the bell for me was the answers in Genesis, and that with these you had answers—real answers—and without these there were no answers either in philosophy or in the religion I had heard preached."[4] Much later he wrote the book *Genesis in Space and Time,* because without the Book of Genesis, nothing else in the Bible holds together or makes sense.

By the leading of God and out of curiosity, on a hot August evening in 1930 he wandered into an old-fashioned tent meeting revival to see what was going on. There he heard the gospel preached according to the Scriptures and as he had learned it to be true from his independent studies. Here he found Christians, people who knew God as he knew him. He went forward at the altar call, when the preacher called for repentant sinners to come forward and accept Christ as Savior. He took the side of God publicly and stood with others who believed in the Christ of the Bible.

When Fran became a Christian, he did so because Christianity was true. It made sense. It was logical. It was a reasonable system that people could talk about and share with others as the only answer to life and the questions life poses. And later he wrote, "The basis for our faith is that certain things are true. The whole man, including the intellect, is to act upon the fact that certain things are true. That, of course, will lead to an experiential relationship with God; but the basis is content, not experience."[5]

From his experience and his studies, he had been able to compare ideas, and he could see what was true and what was false. Christianity was true to life, and it answered the questions life posed. He found that man doesn't invent the questions of life and then invent the answers; rather, man discovers the questions life poses for his generation, and then by the leading of the Holy Spirit he may also discover that the Bible, though written long ago, gives the basic answers. He learns that the Bible, grounded in history, is true in all that it affirms, and that it must be God's revelation to save lost and dying man. Man thinks up the questions of life and then finds that God has already given him the answers in the Bible. For Fran, this was a strong argument for the authority and the reliability of the Bible as a revelation from God (not, however, the only argument in favor of the Bible's inerrancy).

After finding the truth, Fran had to make a choice. He could believe in, trust, and obey Jesus Christ. Or he could turn away and live his own life on his own terms. Fran accepted Jesus Christ as his Savior, and at the same time he made him his Lord. God did not program him to make him into a Christian. God did not overpower him or force him to make a decision against his will. By his grace, God called Francis Schaeffer to be both a Christian and a significant influence in his century, but Fran had to walk willingly, and in spite of great struggles, in the path God chose for him. God led him gently by the compelling truth of his Word. He enlightened him by the power of the Holy Spirit. Fran made a responsible choice to follow Jesus. And then he asked God to help him make all his future choices day by day.

Fran would later say that God had made a significant man in a significant history, and that man can work into history and change history just as God works into history and can change history. Man is responsible before God for the choices he makes, and these choices make a difference throughout eternity.

Shortly after becoming a Christian, he felt called to the Christian ministry, but he knew what a heartbreak this would be to his parents! He knew how antagonistic they would be. How could he convince his parents to accept this vocational turn, when they felt that all ministers were little more than parasites upon society?

1. The quotations by Dr. C. Everett Koop and Dr. Billy Graham were taken from the article, "Dr. Francis A. Schaeffer: God's Man for This Era," by Susan LeGras Davis, *Good News Publishers PIONEER,* Number 133, July-August, 1984, p. 1.

2. Taken from Cal Thomas, "Francis August Schaeffer IV: Crusader for Truth," *The Fundamentalist Journal,* July/August 1984, p. 48.

3. Ibid.

4. Edith Schaeffer, *The Tapestry* (Waco: Word Books, 1981), p. 52. See also the award-winning special memorial edition in the 1984 paperback.

5. Francis Schaeffer, *The New Super-Spirituality,* in *The Complete Works of Francis A. Schaeffer* (Westchester: Crossway Books, 1982), Volume Three, Book Three, p. 391.

2
GROWING IN TRUTH

WHEN FRAN told his parents he planned to be a minister, they fiercely opposed the idea. They wanted him to get a degree in engineering. He quickly discovered that he would have to go against his parents' wishes if he were to study and prepare for the ministry! He chose to obey God rather than man, but this meant real pain in his family relationships. His mother carried an unforgiving bitterness far into his years of ministry and in many ways made life miserable for the entire family.

Through the advice and counsel of some Christian friends and leaders in his church, Fran decided to apply to Hampden-Sydney College in Virginia and begin preministerial studies in the fall of 1931. He had no idea how he would finance his schooling, but he prayed and trusted that if the Lord had called him to the ministry, the Lord would meet his needs. For Fran, this was a practical step of faith in his heavenly Father.

In preparation for college he worked hard studying Latin and German in night school, and during the day he worked equally hard to earn money for school. Fran believed that God would provide for his needs in preparation for the ministry, but he also knew that God expected him to work diligently to prepare himself in every way for his calling—materially, intellectually, and spiritually. Students who later came to L'Abri quickly learned that Dr. Schaeffer expected them to do both intellectual and physical labor as they grew spiritually.

Finally, one early morning in September of 1931, Fran began getting ready to leave for college. A little more than a year had passed since he had publicly accepted Jesus Christ as his Lord and Savior. On the basis of the finished work of Christ, his guilt was gone and he felt joyful to be going to a school where he could learn more about the way upon which he had embarked. But still he didn't have his father's blessing or permission. He did not want to go against the wishes of his father; he felt torn between his love and obligation for his earthly father and his heavenly Father. He sincerely felt a personal struggle between God's call to the ministry and his father's call to work beside him.

His dad met him at the door one day as he was going off to work, and he commanded his son directly: "I don't want a son who is a minister, and—I don't want you to go."[1] After praying in the cellar and seeking the Lord's will again, Fran went upstairs to see his dad, who had waited to hear his decision. He said, "Dad, I've got to go. . . ."[2] With that, his father slammed the door in anger behind him, but he also called out that he would pay Fran's school expenses for the first half year.

Years later his dad did become a Christian, but if Fran had not made the decision to follow his heavenly Father, no matter what the personal cost in family and friends, his own earthly father might never have found

Christ as his Savior. In his decision to follow Christ only, Fran had also made a choice for his own children, that he would raise them in a Christian home, even though at that time he probably had no thought of all the ramifications of his decision. Literally thousands of others might never have come to a Bible-believing Christian faith if he had not chosen at that one moment in history to put God first in his life no matter what the personal cost. The decisions we make *now* cause ripples throughout eternity!

His arrival at Hampden-Sydney was not easy either. He was from the working class, a poor blue-collar worker; his student peers were from the aristocracy. He was a Northerner, a Yankee, and they were Southern gentlemen. He was studying to be a minister—from a heartfelt concern for people and with a real intellectual conviction about God and what it meant to serve only him. Many of his fellow students didn't want to be around a person who might afflict their consciences as they threw off the religious morality of their home life.

He was placed purposely on a dormitory floor with students who were especially antagonistic to ministerial students, particularly to those with strong religious convictions. As a freshman student, he was picked on unmercifully and physically abused, until the day he rose to the occasion and dished out a little of what he had been receiving! Before long, he had won the admiration of his professors and fellow students.

Even at this time in his life, he felt he needed to show Christian firmness according to the holiness of God. He never claimed perfection, and his standing for the holiness of God was not on the basis of his own merits, but on the basis of the character of a holy God. His own life did, however, show substantial consistency in holy living, or he would never have had an impact upon his peers; he would have appeared to be a hypocrite. When one studies Schaeffer's life, one finds a substantial consistency between his life and his words *throughout* his life, and this is one of the primary reasons for his success as an evangelist.

While he was standing for the holiness of God, he also believed that he needed to show forth love and compassion for those who did not know the God of the Bible. At one point in his college career he made a pact with some of the students that if they would attend church with him on Sunday morning, he would help them to their beds after a Saturday night carousal. In this way he hoped that they might hear and respond to the gospel. Asked if he minded doing this, he simply said, "Oh, it gave me time to keep up with my studies while the others were out." He started a short prayer meeting and Bible study on his dorm floor, and many of the students found this helpful. He kept it short to hold their interest. At graduation he was given an award for being the most outstanding Christian on campus during his four years.

For Fran, Christianity was never just an intellectual theory or a game to play; it was a life to be lived, a Lord to love and serve, and a message to spread to as many as possible. Even after he became a noted Christian thinker, he never just "theologized" for the sake of discussion. He believed that theological discussion could become just another exciting game to some people, and that it could actually be a barrier to real and honest discipleship.

Consistent with his concern for all people, even in 1931, when he was only nineteen years old, he walked through the woods every week to teach the Bible to a group of poor black children. He knew no barriers of race or color in Jesus Christ, and he lived on that basis, even when many had a deep-seated prejudice against their black brothers and sisters. He was going to these little black children because he loved them and saw them as individuals before God, but at the same time, probably unconsciously, he was making a social statement regarding every Christian's responsibility to those who are different in some respects from themselves, but who are still created in the image of God. This early concern for all people, this love for all of God's children from all backgrounds, was one of the strengths of his entire ministry. His consistent attitude in this regard made its impact upon L'Abri, actually making L'Abri a possibility, as people have come to L'Abri literally from the ends of the earth.

Among his other college activities, he became president of the Literary Society and entered debates. He was on the cabinet of the Christian Student Association and a member of the Ministerial Association. He was a member of Theta Kappa Nu fraternity and fulfilled his obligations to the fraternity, but after that experience he resolved never again to join another secular organization! He said that at some point secular organizations always come at odds with the Christian faith and practice.

Fran met his wife-to-be, Edith Rachel Merritt Seville, on June 26, 1932. He had finished his first year at Hampden-Sydney College and had returned home to work for the summer. They met one evening at the First Presbyterian Church.

Edith was born into a very different world from Fran's, and her parents had a very different outlook from his. Her parents were of Irish-American ancestry, with one of her ancestors being a Revolutionay War veteran from England (who had fought on the American side). Her father, George Hugh Seville, was born in 1876 and lived until 1977. Her mother, Jessie Maude Merritt, was born in 1874. Her mother had planned with her first husband, Walter Greene, to enter the mission field with the China Inland Mission. But after one year of marriage she was bereaved of both her husband and baby boy in 1895. Being a woman of courage and devotion, she left on her own to attend Toronto Bible College and then became a missionary with the China Inland Mission, leaving for Shanghai in 1899. In China she was diligently pursued by George Hugh Seville, who, after an adventurous courtship within Chinese propriety, married her on March 29, 1905.

Edith Seville was born in China, the fourth child, on November 3, 1914. She spent her first four years of life in the missionary compound, a very precocious and strong-willed child. She observed the missionary work of her parents in the China Inland Mission, learned the language, and evaluated the culture that she called home. She even learned how to drink tea with rice packed in one cheek, not to be touched by the tea. Missionary work and Christian service were a part of her life and the life of her family. Her cousin Marion, for example, served as a missionary to Egypt. When she died she had managed to save and give in her will $20,000 for the building of Farel House for L'Abri in Switzerland. At Farel House many Egyptians, among others, would study, and some would become Christians.

The educational interests and background of her father played an important role in Edith's life. He had studied at Allegheny Theological Seminary from 1900-1902, before going to China. He returned with his family in the summer of 1919 and continued his work with the C.I.M. He became an editor of the magazine *China's Millions,* and later was pastor of the Presbyterian Church in Newburgh, New York. He was well-read in biblical and theological areas, and was friends with such great Christian leaders as Robert Dick Wilson and J. Gresham Machen, professors at Princeton Theological Seminary before the founding of Westminster Theological Seminary. When Edith wanted to study and prepare herself for making an able defense of the Christian faith, while still in high school, her father gave her the books of these two great men to study.

Edith cannot remember a time when she was not a Christian. This is not to say she was perfect, but she can remember no time when Jesus was not both her Savior and Lord. She loved the Bible and she loved to pray. With the example of her parents, the memory of J. Hudson Taylor's missionary endeavors in the China Inland Mission, and with the opportunity to meet world-renowned Christian scholars who stood up courageously and sacrificially for the faith, she was being prepared by God for the work that he was to call her to do with Francis Schaeffer. Her completely opposite childhood would give balance and stability to his work and give him an understanding of the great variety of ways people come to Christ. She would know how to rear a family in a Christian home while showing Christian hospitality. She would do those things that would make for a balanced Christian family, showing each family member that he or she was cared for individually. There were many things about a Christian family and witness that Fran simply had not personally experienced in his home. Their backgrounds would complement each other's strengths and weaknesses.

By the time Edith was in high school, she was already fighting for the truth of the Christian faith. Sometimes the arena was the school classroom, and at other times it was in the Presbyterian Church. The church youth meetings were often quite radical in their denial of Christian truth and equally devoid of spiritual benefit.

One Sunday evening a Unitarian, a former member of her church, came to speak on why he denied the Christian position regarding God, Jesus Christ, and the truth of the Bible. Following the talk, Edith started to stand up and argue against him, using the materials she had been studying. But before she could rise, a boy she had never seen before began to refute what had just been said. Until that moment Edith hadn't known of anyone else in her church who believed as she did. When the boy finished, Edith stood up and made her position plain. The boy didn't know that there was anyone else in his church who believed as *he* did!

The girl had just moved to town, and the boy had just returned from one year of college. That night, following the meeting, Francis Schaeffer and Edith Seville were formally introduced. They had met on the field of combat, and they were fighting on the same side, both with much intellectual acumen and passion. That night in June 1932 there began a partnership of learning and teaching that would mark their work together and eventually come to be known simply as "L'Abri," a shelter and a family for those who had lost their faith and subsequently any meaning for living, but who came to find salvation through Jesus Christ.

Edith and Francis began a nonstop discussion and

correspondence from the moment they met. While Fran was finishing the next three years at Hampden-Sydney College, they wrote each other every day. Their romance was a sharing of spiritual truths as well as personal truths. It was Edith who encouraged Fran to read J. Gresham Machen's *Christianity and Liberalism,* and then they discussed it.

While Fran was in school preparing for the ministry, Edith attended Beaver College for Women, commuting every day to save money. Her major was home economics, but with a wide and extensive curriculum that covered many different practical areas. Her Christian commitment led her to begin meetings of the League of Evangelical Students on campus. These were also difficult times, as she had to face the challenges of those intellectuals who had embraced and were promoting the communist positions regarding religion and social concerns.

Many things can be learned from their correspondence during this time. For example, Edith idealized that Fran was going to be one of the greatest men of God. She wanted to be his companion in *everything.* Fran remarked about the death of a fine professor and said that he would have been even greater "if he had had love in his life." At another time, they both rededicated their lives to God, to the point of being willing to part with each other if that were God's will. They were both reading *Daily Light* each day, to have this biblical and spiritual experience in common while apart.

In March of 1935 Fran applied for admission to seminary. He was an A student and was to graduate second in his class, magna cum laude with a B.A. degree. All was not an easy glide from college to seminary, however; they were not isolated from the winds of change in their denomination. By April Dr. J. Gresham Machen was on trial for his work in independent missions, and this was a real matter of prayer for Fran and Edith too. The result of that trial would affect their own future in the liberal Presbyterian Church. When they finally learned that summer that Dr. Machen had been defrocked, Fran wrote immediately and resigned from the Northern Presbyterian Church and went under care as a seminary student with the Presbytery of the Presbyterian Church of America.

In looking back forty years later upon his withdrawal from the liberal Presbyterian Church, he said he was glad he had not spent the last forty years fighting a rearguard battle and being looked upon as a maverick within his denomination. Because we have just so much energy, he believed that if he had stayed, he would never have been able to achieve what he had. Because he recognized that the Church is the Body of Christ and not just another organization, he advised, "I personally would not belong to any denomination where there was no hope of recovering the bureaucracy or the seminaries" for Jesus Christ.

Fran and Edith were grateful for the Bible that gave them truth—objective truth with absolute standards. The Bible enabled them to develop principles whereby they could, with a sound conscience, take a stand in opposition to the Northern Presbyterian Church. As early as 1935, however, Fran also recognized the need in his life for the sweetness, gentleness, and kindness that comes from love as one stands at the same time for truth. He had to battle his temper all of his life, but he did develop that kindness that he sought. In all his struggles and decisions, Edith stood with him in prayer and with sound counsel. They faced life's challenges together and with their God, knowing that they could trust the promises in his Word.

Fran graduated in early June from Hampden-Sydney College, and he and Edith were married on July 6, 1935. That first summer together they were church camp counselors in Michigan and began an early work together with children. This was a time for learning more about each other, both their perfections and their imperfections, their need to deal with Fran's temper, that could flame very easily, and with Edith's strong will, once she had made a decision.

Later they deplored the many divorces among Christian leaders and the many breakups of Christian homes. They saw this as real disobedience to the Word of God, as well as a poor testimony. When speaking of marriage, Edith often declared that marriage is a 90 percent and 10 percent relationship. You give 90 percent and the other gives 10 percent, and then the other gives 90 percent and you give 10 percent, when you are unable to give what is needed. After Fran's death she reflected upon marriage and illness: "Pain and discomfort need to be shared. One person may be the well one, and one the ill one, but both are involved, which, after all, is what the oneness of marriage—the 'for better and worse, in sickness and in health'—is all about. In spite of being two separate persons, there is a reality of sharing life together which the modern 'scream of rights' or 'scream for independence' knows nothing about!"[3]

Being creative, Edith paid for much of Fran's schooling at Westminster Theological Seminary by working as a seamstress. He would study late in the evening, and she would stay up and sew in order to share with him the ideas he was learning. In this way, and also with her own avid reading, she was able to acquire the equivalent of a seminary education without the benefit of formal classroom attendance. Later she would receive an honorary doctor's degree. One can see from her later work as a writer and conversationalist that their times of study and discussion together were to be for her able ministry as well as his. They learned the importance of discussing ideas together, and this became a vital part of their family life as well as the life of L'Abri.

During their years in seminary and following, two problems plagued the Schaeffers as they sought greater reality in their Christian faith. The first problem became a keynote of Dr. Schaeffer's teaching and private conversations only after his hayloft experience in the 1950's; that is, *Christians must always stand for holiness and love at the same time.* He came to believe that this can never be done in a person's own strength. It can be done only in the power and through the ministry of the Holy Spirit in our individual lives. His many battles with his own imperfections drove him closer and closer to Christ and the indwelling Holy Spirit. He faced the challenge to make "a simultaneous exhibition of the holiness of God and the love of God." Prior to his hayloft experience, he stood for God's holiness and for orthodoxy, but without love, and this was a serious problem in his relationship with others even in his churches in America.

The second problem that bothered them was the view that almost every action or decision that people make is in some way predetermined or caused by God. In this view, choice is not real choice. Pushed to its extreme, this view says prayer doesn't make any real difference, because in some mysterious way God has already determined what he is going to do or not do anyway. With this view, we cannot pray, making our requests known to God, and expect these requests to make any real difference in history. People are shut in to praying only prayers of thanksgiving or confession.

L'Abri was built to demonstrate the reality of answered prayer and to show that we have every right to make requests of God as we seek his direction for our lives. Later, Dr. Schaeffer carefully wrote, "God, being nondetermined, created man as a nondetermined person. This is a difficult idea for anyone thinking in twentieth-century terms, because most twentieth-century thinking sees man as determined."[4] At Westminster they faced a particular form of theological determinism, whereas twentieth-century secular man thinks in terms of being determined by chemical factors or psychological factors or sociological factors.

While in seminary and following graduation, they had to deal with problems from these two perspectives in very practical ways as they sought to demonstrate the presence of God and the truth of God to their generation by their lives and by their prayers.

Later one theological professor, who for years often publicly criticized Schaeffer's way of helping people become Christians, retired and then wrote a long critical treatment of Schaeffer's view of Christian faith and evangelism. Dr. Schaeffer responded privately to some within L'Abri: "I would hate to think that I might spend my retirement doing something like that!" Still, he kept all of this man's works available for study at L'Abri, while withdrawing his own tapes that discussed this man's views and their disagreements. Dr. Schaeffer seldom responded publicly to his critics; he simply didn't have the time, and he preferred to discuss ideas. To clarify his views, however, he did add a special appendix on the ways he presented Christian truth, in the first volume of his *Complete Works.* After he began L'Abri, Dr. Schaeffer preferred to deal with his critics on a private and a personal level through careful correspondence.

After Fran's second year at Westminster Theological Seminary in Philadelphia, another split took place within the new Presbyterian Church, following the death of Dr. Machen. Fran left with Professor MacRae and others to help form Faith Seminary in Wilmington, Delaware.

The summer of 1937 found Fran and Edith busily getting the living accommodations ready for staff and students to open Faith Seminary in the fall. Here Fran's background stood him in good stead as he salvaged old bathroom fixtures from junk yards for the remodeled apartments he was in charge of restoring. He also arranged for his capable father-in-law, Dr. George Seville, to join the faculty and teach missions and introductory Greek. He continued to teach there for seventeen years, until he was eighty. Fran and Edith's first child, Priscilla, was born on June 18, 1937, in the midst of their busy preparations of founding a new school.

Fall seminary classes began on time in the Faith Bible Presbyterian Church. Fran was the first student to enroll. He graduated in the first graduating class, and he was the first pastor to be ordained in the Bible Presbyterian Church. All through his seminary course he made an A average. What kind of future did God have in mind for this bright and promising seminary graduate? Where would he send the Schaeffers as he nurtured and prepared them?

1. *The Tapestry,* p. 60.

2. Ibid., p. 62.

3. *L'Abri Family Letter,* July 17, 1984, p. 8, by Edith Schaeffer.

4. *The God Who Is There* in *The Complete Works,* Volume One, Book One, pp. 112-113.

3
SHARING THE TRUTH

FOLLOWING GRADUATION and ordination, Fran, Edith, and eleven-month-old Priscilla left for Grove City, Pennsylvania. Fran was to be the new pastor of the Covenant Presbyterian Church. The new church consisted of eighteen adults, and on their first Sunday morning no children were present. The parents believed their children needed to be in a larger Sunday school than their new church could provide.

In their first church, Edith learned to pray without ceasing for her husband while he was in the pulpit. As the wife of the pastor, she felt this was one of her most important responsibilities.

They worked hard together. Fran prepared hot dog roasts in the park to meet new boys and eventually win them and their families to Christ and the church. Edith helped organize and taught in their summer Vacation Bible School. Their first summer, in a church with no Sunday school, seventy-nine pupils attended the first day of Vacation Bible School, and by its end over one hundred were present. Leading people to accept Jesus

Christ as their Lord and Savior was a strong emphasis of their work, and some people became Christians at their first attempt to hold a Vacation Bible School.

Not all their efforts were so successful, however. They tried to reach out to the college students at Grove City College, but failed. They little realized at the time that they would soon be reaching college students from all over the world through L'Abri.

Just as prayer was always an important part of their own life together, Fran began a praying family in a small way in the church by asking a bedfast woman, the wife of an elder, if she would pray for special needs. He would go to her house and share his prayer requests with her, and he always felt that her prayers were an important reason for many wonderful things that happened at Grove City.

Their church grew so fast under his ministry that in less than three years a new building was built, and the membership reached 110. This seems almost incredible when we consider that Fran was a only a recent graduate from seminary. In the midst of this success, however, with new people coming to church every Sunday, one of Fran's elders suggested that after three years a minister ought to move on to a new church. He felt that Fran had said probably all he had to say!

On May 28, 1941, their second daughter, Susan, was born. A few months later Fran began serving as the associate pastor of the Bible Presbyterian Church of Chester, Pennsylvania. Dr. A. L. Lathem was the senior pastor.

Prior to his working with Dr. Lathem, and as they were in the process of building in Grove City, Fran had also been busy building up the Bible Presbyterian Church as a whole. He had served as moderator of the

Great Lakes Presbytery of the Bible Presbyterian Church, a real honor and responsibility for such a young man.

Fran served in Chester for less than two years. He helped them complete their building program, but he didn't want to be involved in building any more buildings where he felt no more were really needed. His expertise in building was needed when he first arrived in Chester, as his education in the trades enabled him to help with the building plans and gave him the ability to climb up on the scaffolding to work with the members of the church, who were volunteering their time after work to do much of the actual construction.

In this church of more than five hundred members, Fran's background enabled him to converse with shipyard workers as well as farmers, with the practical working man as well as the intellectual. He came to believe that people around the world ask essentially the same questions about life and about God and that we just need to learn their language. Learning another's language is a part of what it means to love them. He never looked down upon another person's calling. He did insist, however, that people be sure they were called of God to be a dockworker or a teacher, a carpenter or a preacher. The important thing was living as a consistent Christian in whatever vocation God has called you to, and realizing that God can place us where he wants to in the spiritual battles we are called to fight.

One reason Fran could deal with difficulties and unexpected "moves" in life, without being completely shattered by them, was that he knew we are in a spiritual battle. The battle between Satan and God in the unseen world affects us. We can be wounded in the battle, and we can wound Satan in the battle. In the spiritual warfare we fight, Jesus Christ is the King, and he has the right to place us in the battlefield where he sees fit, and where he believes we can do the most good for the Kingdom. For this reason, Fran tried not to complain against God, but he looked upon his difficult times and difficult places as opportunities to give the most to God and learn the most from God in the midst of a spiritual battle.

By 1942 Fran's father had become a Christian. He saw in Fran's and Edith's lives the practical application of the Christian faith, something he hadn't seen before, as Christianity had always appeared to be irrelevant to life. Fran showed him that the ministry can be practical and that pastors do not have to be parasites upon society.

People of whatever place or position in life were important to Fran. While in Chester, he began to work with a child with Down's syndrome, whose parents could ill afford special education. Later, another child with Down's syndrome joined them. Children with special problems had a special place in his heart, and this is one of the reasons he worked so hard against abortion and infanticide.

At Chester Fran continued to obey the Scriptures in everything. One day a very poor family was told that their little girl had an incurable tongue disease, one that would take her life. Her parents asked Fran to anoint her with oil and pray for her healing. He did so in obedience to the Scriptures, and she was miraculously healed.[1]

He believed that Bible-believing Christians should practice living in the supernatural world. For him, Christianity was not just a way of thinking; Christianity was a special way of living based upon a special way of thinking. He acted upon the basis that the Bible was true, and the result was many experiences of answered prayer. He strived to maintain a close and personal relationship with God, so God could use him in any way he saw fit.

During his long ministry, he prayed at other times for people to be healed; sometimes people were healed and at other times they were not. He never claimed to be a faith healer; he only tried to be obedient to the Word of God. Just as humility and the primary call to preach and teach prompted Jesus not to emphasize his healing ministry, so Fran felt called primarily to preach the truth and emphasize the practice of God's Word in his generation. He quietly demonstrated the truth of Proverbs 11:30, "The fruit of the righteous is a tree of life, and he who wins souls is wise."

All through their lives Fran and Edith combined prayer with obedient hard work. Their consistency in believing God's Word, while praying and working hard, was mightily blessed by God. They became a clear and open channel for the flow of his grace.

Fran was low-key about his accomplishments. He was not a sensationalist. For example, in a group discussion someone asked him if he believed in demon possession and the casting out of demons. In his characteristically careful way, he replied that he could not definitely say that he had ever seen a person who was demon possessed; however, in L'Abri some people have come to Christ from completely pagan backgrounds, and as these people were accepting Christ as Savior, in prayer, sometimes things would begin to fly off the walls, and strange things would happen.

By faith, Fran and Edith lived in the presence of God. They lived in both the natural and the supernatural world. Fran taught that just as Jesus Christ lives in those who have come to him by faith, and just as he also lives in the presence of his Father in heaven, so we too are called to live in the Father's presence. Faith is believing and trusting in God, and faith is also living in the supernatural *now,* in real communication with God.

Fran believed in the specific promises of God given in the Bible, and in faith he acted upon those promises. But he also knew that God sometimes had his own reasons for not answering his prayers for healing or other requests. He saw no inconsistency between praying for healing and at the same time taking the best medicines doctors could provide. He believed in using all of God's gifts (the gifts of faith, prayer, and medicine, for example) in the battle to defeat Satan, sickness, and death. Trouble and illnesses were not always a sign of a lack of faith; neither do we have to throw away our medicine to prove our faith before God will heal us. Often our troubles are the results of living in a fallen world. Perfection will not come until the next world, after Christ has returned.

Francis and Edith Schaeffer were deeply spiritual and practical people. Their prayers were practical expressions of their desire to honor God and know his will. One evening as they were seeking to know God's definite leading regarding their next church move, Edith was praying for some clear evidence that they were to move to St. Louis, Missouri. All of a sudden, in the midst of her prayer, the Holy Spirit impressed upon her some new words to an old hymn. These words, an expression of submission to the will of God, convinced her that God had answered her prayer for guidance, and that indeed they were to go to the Bible Presbyterian Church in St. Louis. Prayer, reason, and the experience of answered prayer enabled God to guide their lives by his choices as well as theirs.

In 1943, the year his father died, Fran began a very joyful work in St. Louis. He and his family were comfortable in every way and loved the people and the work. Forty years later, some of those members would still visit them as they came to them for help or counsel while patients at the Mayo Clinic. Fran would typically preach two sermons on Sunday and give a Bible study at their Wednesday night prayer meeting. They started a children's Bible class in their basement, and Fran taught the church women how to do the same thing. Before long, twenty such classes were being held in the basements of church members throughout the city. This was actually the beginning of what would later be called "Children for Christ," a work they would soon take to the churches of Europe. One of their former church members in St. Louis said of Fran's work there: "He worked hard, and he worked the people hard!"

During his time in St. Louis, Fran worked in the American Council of Christian Churches. Since he was a part of their leadership, he began a council of churches to include the Bible-believing groups in the St. Louis area. His social concern expressed itself again when he wrote a pamphlet to combat Hitler's antisemitism. "The Bible-believing Christian and the Jew" was distributed by the thousands in the midst of the war years.

Deborah Ann was born in St. Louis on May 3, 1945. By the time she was two years old, Fran was to make his first trip to Europe on behalf of the American Council of Christian Churches and the Independent Board for Presbyterian Foreign Missions, the board begun by J. Gresham Machen. He was to be gone for three months to find out the situation of the churches following the war and to warn them about the theological dangers that their students might face in some of the American seminaries and Bible colleges. One of his formal titles for this trip was "The American Secretary, Foreign Relations Department of The American Council of Christian Churches." The letters he wrote from Europe were carefully recopied by Edith for publication. Studying the state of the church and the state of the nations, and writing for publication about his many observations, began many years prior to L'Abri and his first books.

During his ninety days in Europe, he met key Christian leaders and spoke at various times before many diverse groups of people. This gave him a real sense of being a part of a greater heritage than he had realized before. He marveled at the various sites of the Reformation, and he felt called to help carry forward the Reformation principles. He quickly learned that the state of the church in Europe was horrible! Of sixty pastors, for example, in the Geneva State Church, only two or three were Bible-believing Christians. Some of the key people he met felt definitely that they ought to separate themselves and their churches from Karl Barth and the ecumenical movement.

He spoke at meetings and hoped to help develop an International Council of Christian Churches to stand firm for the Bible and be united in a front against the liberal takeover of the traditional churches. In their life story, *The Tapestry,* Edith made the observation that is characteristic of their thinking together along these lines: "What a variety of wars there are, and what varied forms of devastation. Inadequate and watered-down food depletes physical bodies, but inadequate, watered-down, and even poisoned spiritual food endangers spiritual life."[2]

The World Council of Churches was just getting off the ground in a big way when Fran was touring Europe. It was formally founded in 1948, with headquarters in Geneva. Today, we don't think as much as we should about the blatant and vicious worldwide subversion of the churches by World Council leaders, but Fran clearly remembered the words of Dr. Visser't Hooft at the Oslo Young People's Conference in Norway in July of 1947, one year before the founding of the World Council. Visser't Hooft challenged the young people to confront the Bible-believing Christians in their churches in order to "drive the greyheads out" to have more churches in the World Council. On July 26, 1947, Fran went to hear the American theologian Reinhold Niebuhr speak. He believed that in that speech Niebuhr was using the ideas of Karl Barth to create a socialistic interpretation of Christianity. Of the World Council Conference itself, he lamented, "The whole Conference makes me desperately lonely for some Christian contact."[3]

Schaeffer's spiritual depth at the time is illustrated in a letter he wrote to his wife, for he told of his concern for his people in St. Louis. "Often in the midst of other things, one or another person comes to my mind, and I pray immediately for that one then."[4] This loving concern for people, and the practical expression of that love through prayer when apart, always characterized Fran's ministry.

He was not concerned about theological and intellectual issues apart from their impact on the Christian faith. He felt there should be experience and emotion in the Christian faith, but that experience and emotion could not be the *basis* for Christian faith. Christian faith must be based upon the Bible, which is true in all that it affirms. Christian faith is truth that must be shared. Christians live in faith, knowing prayer makes a difference.

When he went to Europe, he had practically no contacts and no names. He went with the continuing prayer that God would take him to the people he would have him meet. God answered his prayer. He was led to people deeply interested in helping to form the International Council of Christian Churches. And upon his return home he received many requests to come back and help the embattled theologians, churches, and pastors of Europe.

One of the most unusual providential occurrences of Fran's life took place upon his return from Europe. The airplane in which he was flying across the Atlantic suddenly developed engine trouble and plunged three thousand feet. A ham radio operator who knew Fran was crossing the Atlantic at the time heard the distress signals and called Edith and the children at home. They gathered together as a family and prayed, knowing that Fran was scheduled to be on that plane. Fran, of course, was praying too. The engines miraculously started again, and Fran arrived home safely. When he got off the plane, he heard the pilots say that they couldn't understand how those engines could have started again, that it was impossible. Fran told them very matter-of-factly, "I know how they started; my Father started them." Proverbs 15:29 states: "The Lord is far from the wicked but he hears the prayers of the righteous."

His first trip to Europe was to be one of his greatest spiritual experiences. It wasn't all negative as he thought of the huge battle for truth that was ahead. He thanked

God for the unity of the true Church of Christ around the world. He felt it crucial for the true churches to separate themselves from the modern forms of unbelief and paganism that characterized liberalism. Later he wrote:

> Nowhere is practicing the truth more important than in the area of religious cooperation. If I say that Christianity is really eternal truth, and the liberal theologian is wrong—so wrong that he is teaching that which is contrary to the Word of God—and then on any basis (including for the sake of evangelism) I am willing publicly to act as though that man's religious position is the same as my own, I have destroyed the practice of truth which my generation can *expect* from me and which it will *demand* of me if I am to have credibility. How will we have *credibility* in a relativistic age if we practice religious cooperation with men who in their books and lectures make very plain that they believe nothing (or practically nothing) of the content set forth in Scripture?[5]

When he made his reports to the Independent Board and to the American Council, everyone was satisfied with his work, but Fran was burned out. He didn't feel he could ever travel again, ever answer the phone again, or ever have another meeting. In the midst of his months of recovery, the Independent Board asked him to be their missionary to Europe.

It was a real struggle for the family to decide to make this radical change from their happy life in St. Louis. But Fran was needed to help establish the new International Council of Christian Churches. Fran was needed to travel and speak for six months prior to the first meeting of the International Council, to be held in Amsterdam in August of 1948. It was essential that they leave for Europe in February, less than six months from the time of his exhausting tour.

What could a family of five do, sent to the whole continent of Europe so soon after a major war had brought its devastation? What could they do right in the midst of a massive reconstruction effort? What battles could two dedicated, Bible-believing Christians win in the struggle for truth that was facing the church and the world? What could Fran do when rising German theological stars (such as Karl Barth and Paul Tillich) were making such a tremendous impact with their ideas upon the world theological scene, the seminaries, the pastors, and the churches? How would they inspire people to faith and action, a people who were exhausted, and who after the war seemed to want only peace and unity at any price? "When the foundations are being destroyed, what can the righteous do?" (Psalm 11:3).

1. See James 5:13-15.

2. *The Tapestry,* p. 256.

3. Ibid., p. 258.

4. Ibid., p. 261.

5. *Two Contents, Two Realities* in *The Complete Works,* Volume Three, Book Four, p. 411.

4
FIGHTING FOR TRUTH

IN THEIR LIFE together, Francis and Edith Schaeffer were to experience over and over again the truth of Romans 8:28, that all things work for good to those who love God, and who are called according to his purpose. They were called according to the purpose of God to go to Europe when they did, but that also meant that Satan would increase the fierceness of his attacks upon them. Going to Switzerland was the beginning of an intense spiritual warfare that would last all their lives. Satan might afflict them and hurt them with real pain or lasting scars, but in everything God would work for his good as well as theirs.

An expression of the gracious love of God occurred when Priscilla was placed in the Philadelphia Children's Hospital shortly before they were to leave for Europe. Her doctor thought she wasn't really sick, but she was actually getting worse and worse. But then Dr. C. Everett Koop saw her "by accident," and noted that she needed surgery as soon as possible. Hence, as early as 1948, the Schaeffers came to meet Dr. Koop, who had just become a Christian a few weeks before. He was destined to play a large part in their lives and in the life of L'Abri. During Priscilla's surgery, Fran was serving as the moderator of the Bible Presbyterian Church Conference which was meeting in Nashville, Tennessee. His thoughtfulness of his daughter at this time made a lasting impression upon Dr. Koop, as he saw the practical expression of the Christian faith that characterized Schaeffer's ministry. Fran sent his daughter a telegram with a Scripture to help calm her fears in his absence.

The Schaeffers arrived in Europe when Fran was thirty-six years old, and he would spend the next thirty-six years there as a missionary. When they arrived in Amsterdam, Schaeffer became the recording secretary for the founding conference of the International Council of Christian Churches. Here the most important event to take place, as it related to the future of L'Abri, was his meeting a young art critic, Hans Rookmaaker. Rookmaaker was captivated by Fran's understanding of the Christian faith and its relationship to art as they talked outside the conference during one of the meetings. This "chance" conversation began a lasting friendship between the Rookmaakers and the Schaeffers, lasting until Hans' sudden death in 1977.

Following the conference, the Schaeffers moved to Lausanne, where Fran began to contact all the people he had met the year before. "Children for Christ" began in earnest, as Bible studies were written and sent all over Europe to be translated into many different languages. The Rookmaakers even began work in teaching and translating the lessons.

Liberalism and Barthianism so dominated the churches of Europe that children were not being taught the Bible from the viewpoint that it is really true—true in the historical areas as well as in the religious and theological areas. The Children for Christ materials were written to be used in homes and churches to provide a Christian alternative to the current teaching in the churches.

A variety of councils of churches and synods all over Europe needed to be studied and evaluated by Schaeffer regarding future relationships with them. In the summer of 1949, for example, he was asked to attend the Reformed Ecumenical Synod in Amsterdam for two weeks, to determine their stand on Bible-believing Christianity. Here he was disappointed and had to report to the Bible Presbyterian Church that they should not become a member. He counseled that churches and ministers in America should be warned about the synod's rejection of historic, orthodox Christianity.

After living in a very tiny apartment in Lausanne for several months, the Schaeffers rented a chalet in Champery for the summer. Here in Chalet des Frenes they entertained a host of people going to the Second Plenary Congress of the International Council of Christian Churches, which was held in August 1950. Fran himself spoke at the Congress on "The New Modernism (Neoorthodoxy) and the Bible." He had visited with Karl Barth prior to the meeting to make sure his interpretation of Barth was accurate, and the speech was later published as an article.

In Chalet des Frenes, Fran was also to write his first book, *Basic Bible Studies.* He had met a medical doctor who was not a Christian, and he had asked him to read the Bible. The doctor replied, "Oh, I don't have time to do that, and I wouldn't understand it anyway." So Fran proposed, "If I write a brief Bible study for you each week, will you read through it with your Bible?" The doctor said he would, so each week Fran dictated the studies to Edith, who typed them up with multiple carbon copies, and each week Fran gave a copy to the doctor. As others wanted the study too, the carbons were passed out. When all of them were gone, Edith typed them up again with multiple carbons, and these were given away. Finally, they were able to mimeograph the book. It was published by Tyndale House in 1972.

Fran's interest and concern for the arts had been developed long before the founding of L'Abri. In America the Schaeffers had spent many Saturdays with their children in the art museums of St. Louis, teaching them how to appreciate and evaluate art. Sometimes the children would sit and draw the pictures as they studied them. But with Rookmaaker to stimulate his interest and with Fran seeing the need for more Christian involvement in the arts, even as he toured museums all over Europe, he began to promote more avidly the arts as a valid enterprise for Christian involvement. Fran loved life, and very often as he was returning home following a Bible study he had given, he would stop at a museum to study art and history.

Schaeffer was also concerned about "The Separated Movement" as early as 1950, when he began to warn of the danger of getting discouraged with the battle and then compromising with the enemy or withdrawing from the conflict. He also warned against becoming cold and hard of heart as one served the Lord, of failing to recognize that the Lord's work requires self-denial, self-sacrifice, and hard work. He strongly emphasized the need to produce scholarly material as well as warm devotional material. He saw a real danger that the Bible-believing people involved in the battle for truth might lose the love that God commands us to have for one another. He wrote, "There is a danger of developing in our age of necessary contending, a will to win, rather than a will to be right. . . . Our daily prayer should be that our loving Lord will keep His arms so about us that we will neither waver in the fight nor allow the Devil to destroy us from within."[1]

Later, he wrote in *True Spirituality:*

> In the midst of being right, if self is exalted, my fellowship with God can be destroyed. It is not wrong to be right, nor to say that wrong is wrong, but it is wrong to have the wrong attitude in being right, and to forget that my relationship with my fellow men must always be personal and as equals. If I really love man as I love myself, I will long to see him be what he could be on the basis of Christ's work, for that is what I want or what I should want for myself on the basis of Christ's work.[2]

This emphasis characterized all of his life, as well as his last years. The year before he died he said his son had asked him, "Dad, do you think we will win?" And he had to reply, "I don't know, but at least we have fought for what is right. It is not whether we can win or lose, but whether or not we are faithful, loyal, and true to the Lord Jesus Christ." Schaeffer fought on the right sides of the battles of his day, and he tried to do so with love and out of respect for the holiness of God and the truth of the Scriptures. This was also his goal in his final book, *The Great Evangelical Disaster,* which some who did not know him, but who disagreed with him about the truth of Christianity, tried to dismiss as simply "bitterness in his later years."

In 1950, about four years after the liberation of the Germans' prisoners from the death camp Dachau, the Schaeffers went to Dachau to teach a two-week Vacation Bible School for the American children of the soldiers stationed there. This was a moving experience as they saw the actual gas chambers and torture cells run by the German medical doctors before everything was cleaned up and made into a museum. Man's inhumanity to man was graphic, as a displaced persons camp was still being occupied as late as four years after the war. The Schaeffers would return there again for the filming of *Whatever Happened to the Human Race?* as they compared the holocaust to abortion, infanticide, and "mercy killing" now going on with government sanction in many countries around the world. The low view of human life in Germany prior to Hitler's rise to power had prepared the way for the atrocities of his government. Schaeffer knew that the low view of human life in America and around the world, the low view that was allowing the killing of one and one-half million unborn American children every year, would lead to even greater atrocities, especially with all of the new technology we now have, which can be used for either good or evil.

The army officers and the enlisted men at Dachau were impressed at how much their children had learned from only two weeks at Bible School, and this began the Schaeffers' long involvement with military personnel in Europe seeking to know Christ and what it means to obey him in the totality of life. But even during the war, when Schaeffer was a pastor in America, he would talk to the men going overseas and remind them of the ungodly attitude that they could develop when placed in situations where they would have to take the lives of their fellowman. They were not to begin to hate their enemies, but were to realize the need to defend freedom and truth in a fallen world. Fran continued to remind those who fought on the side of right not to aim at "getting rid of the negative at any cost—rather than praying that the negatives might be faced in the proper attitude."[3]

On November 1, 1950, Schaeffer went to Rome to observe the official defining of "The Assumption of Mary," that is, the doctrine of the bodily ascension of Jesus' mother, assuming that she did not die a physical death. It is hard for us to imagine that this doctrine was defined officially only thirty-five years ago. He wrote an article describing the event, with an accompanying explanation regarding how Roman pagan customs had become a part of the Roman Catholic Church. In the paper, one quotation stands out with a bold application for every Christian within the church today: "If, after a careful study of the Bible as God's Word, we Bible-believing Christians are sure we are right, then we are in a battle for the souls of men. . . . The Bible is our authority; do we only march under it as a banner, or do its standards control our lives?"[4]

The year 1951 marked the beginning of a spiritual revival and renewal of Francis Schaeffer's life and ministry. He had been in Europe for three years, and he was facing the crisis of how best to communicate the gospel in a culture that was foreign to him and to a people recently devastated mentally, physically, and spiritually by the World War. Not only was the culture foreign, but most of the so-called Christianity in the churches of Europe was simply not biblical.

At the same time, he was also concerned about the lack of love that was so apparent in many of the orthodox Christian churches he knew. Too many people had developed a hard, inflexible attitude in their standing for the truth. Too much of true Bible-believing Christianity had become unloving and hateful, and he was personally disturbed about the reality of Christianity, if this was the result of it.

He walked and thought in the hayloft of Chalet Bijou in Champery when the weather was bad, and in the mountains when the weather was good. He read his Bible and prayed, and told his wife that he was taking his faith all the way back to his early days of agnosticism (of not knowing whether God was really there or not) to see if there were good and sufficient reasons to be a Christian. From the effort, he renewed his Christian commitment, and this was the real turning point in his life. What he learned from that time was later incorporated into his books *The Church before the Watching World* and *True Spirituality.*

True Spirituality was the one book of his that he read over and over again to remind himself of the reality of the Christian faith and of the importance of balance in the Christian life. It was a book that he felt especially good about in *The Complete Works of Francis A. Schaeffer.*

Obviously, Fran ended his walk with the firm conviction that God is truly, objectively *there* whether we think he is or not, that the Bible is true in all that it affirms, that the Bible applies to the whole of life, and the spiritual reality of the love and holiness of the Holy Spirit must be present in our lives, especially so while fighting for the truth.

During his walk he not only came to some intellectual decisions, but he had the deep spiritual experiences of other great men of God before being called to a greater and more influential work. He found himself walking and praising God; he began to "feel" songs of praise well up from within himself. He began to sing and to write poetry again. He learned what the finished work of Christ meant in present experience; therefore, he began to emphasize more and more that people should become Christians based upon the objective truths of Christian teaching—truths that could be thought through and analyzed again and again based upon new knowledge, but truths that could also bear the weight of thorough investigation. He stressed that a personal, subjective experience and relationship with the Lord Jesus Christ should follow our acceptance of his finished work upon the cross in our behalf.

He has made it clear that he was not speaking about or claiming for himself a "second blessing" or a "second work of grace," neither was he saying that faith is grounded in experience. Christian faith is grounded in the objective revelation of the God of the Bible, but experiencing a relationship with God that continues throughout life should follow a person's new birth. He recognized that his own lack of the reality of the presence of God in his life was related to his ignorance about the meaning of the finished work of Christ in his present life. He began to obey Christ in everything from a real heartfelt love for him, and not from any legalistic motives. Obedience to Christ ceased to be a burden upon his back.

A new door opened to him in the hayloft, a door that led him to acting more upon his knowledge of the Christian faith. He came to realize the necessity of being open to Christ in prayer, so that Jesus Christ could bear his fruit in his life. He learned that if he was to become an agent of God, he must allow Christ to work in him. He believed Christians must know the power of the resurrected Christ in their own lives in the present. He began to insist that the Christian life involves a daily reliance upon the Holy Spirit within us as a constant act of faith. He taught that as Christians we are to think and act upon the promises of Scripture, and ask God to fulfill his promises and bear fruit in our lives for the sake of a world needing to know him. By faith, there should be an ever-increasing, moment by moment experiential relationship with Christ and the whole Trinity. This wonderful spiritual experience of Fran's with his Lord Jesus Christ marked the real beginning of L'Abri, and it shows the truly experiential side of his faith, but it has been too often overlooked by his reviewers and by his critics.

Dr. Schaeffer never again lost his loving relationship with God. Even in his last years he would awake in the morning and sing Christian songs of praise to his God, very unselfconsciously. Sometimes the people downstairs in his home would hear him talking to somebody, but they knew that no one else was upstairs with him. They would listen carefully and hear that he was pausing from his work to pray to his God, his heavenly Father. He was never ashamed of being a Christian or knowing God. One summer day, as he was walking along the beach among the sunbathers, he mentioned to those with him, "All these people are worshiping the wrong 'sun [son],' " and he began to sing softly for all to hear, "Jesus loves me, this I know, for the Bible tells me so." One of his very favorite hymns he often requested that "Jesus Loves Me" by sung during chapel services in Huémoz.

Following his revival experience, he asked Edith a question he has asked others over and over again: "Edith, I wonder what would happen to most churches and Christian work if we awakened tomorrow, and everything concerning the reality and work of the Holy Spirit, and everything concerning prayer, were removed from the Bible. I don't mean just ignored, but actually cut out—disappeared. I wonder how much difference it would make?"[5] He wondered how much Christian work would just continue in its dead sameness, devoid of spiritual power and reality, because those in the work were unaware of the power of the Holy Spirit and the power of prayer. How many Christians had ceased to rely upon the work of God in their lives, and so were doing their work in their own strength? From his speaking on sanctification, Fran later got into trouble with some of the leaders of his denomination. The reaction of these leaders to his speaking about the reality he discovered and his desire to make that reality known were factors in the beginning of the work of L'Abri.

The Schaeffers' early years in Champery, prior to the beginning of L'Abri, saw many girls from finishing schools coming to talk. Many of them became Christians. These girls were from a variety of religious, philosophical, and cultural backgrounds, literally from all over the world. This was a foretaste of the work of L'Abri.

As Fran answered questions, and as many came to believe, they joined the church the Schaeffers had begun in Switzerland, the "International Church, Presbyterian, *Reformé*." This church now has sister congregations in Milan, Ealing, Greatham, and Wimbledon. These congregations are separate from L'Abri, but work with L'Abri. L'Abri is not a church, but many have found that after becoming Christians at L'Abri, they needed a church home until they could find a Bible-believing church wherever they would settle later.

Typically, at the church in Swiss L'Abri, worship will begin at 10:45 A.M., and continue until 12:30 P.M. The children sit on the floor and color quietly or draw, perhaps drawing a picture of the pastor in the pulpit. Children are encouraged to be involved and are included, both in L'Abri and in the International Church.

Francis August Schaeffer V, "Franky," was born August 3, 1952. Two months before his birth, Fran and Edith were in Spain and Portugal, ministering where there was much persecution of Christians by the state, inspired by the Roman Catholic Church. They grieved to see these poor Protestant Christians already under the influence of teaching similar to Karl Barth's. The truth of the Bible was worth being persecuted for, worth standing up for, but the teaching that the Bible was full of error would only destroy these people in the present and in the future.

Their ministry from the beginning was to stand against falsehood and present intellectually defensible reasons for the truth of the Christian faith, when so many were aggressively undermining Christian belief within the church herself. Later, the Schaeffers would join with the Catholics in their stand against abortion, or side with the Pope in his desire to exclude Marxist ideology from Christian teaching or Catholic social efforts, but these were seen as areas where all people should stand together for the sake of the human race. He was consistent in standing against errors in Christian belief wherever he found them.

In 1953 the Schaeffers began their missionary furlough by returning to America. This would hardly be a vacation in any sense of the word, just a change of location. Fran was to teach pastoral theology at Faith Theological Seminary for the year, as well as fulfill a series of speaking engagements around the country to inform the churches about their work.

They had no idea where they would live, and Fran

made this a matter of intensive prayer. In the middle of his asking God to show them a place to live, as he was walking on their balcony in Switzerland, he heard a voice answer him. The voice was so clear that it was as if another person walking with him had spoken three simple words, "Uncle Harrison's house." He wrote to his uncle immediately and received an amazing affirmative answer. His only other experience of hearing a voice during prayer was in response to a prayer asking for God's forgiveness.

Reflecting upon his time in the hayloft, Fran wrote a series of talks he gave many times during his furlough. These were simply titled, "Sanctification I, II, III, IV, V." They stirred a controversy, as Fran pleaded for speaking the truth in love as we stand for the holiness of God. Also, he emphasized the necessity for Christians to rely upon the power of God to minister through them, and not to rely only upon their own strength. At various times Fran encountered misunderstandings in his meetings. There were rumblings about whether or not he should be sent back to Switzerland. When he gave the seminary graduation speech, Edith was approached with the stern warning that the denomination was going to split! Some of the leadership in the synod thought he was making a power play. Edith explained the controversy this way: Fran's message at graduation "had been so contrary to what was normally given of the centrality of pointing out the errors of *others.* Objections came to such statements as: 'There is no source of power for God's people—for preaching or teaching or anything else—except Christ himself. Apart from Christ, anything which seems to be spiritual power is actually the power of the flesh.' "[6]

Fran was awarded the honorary Doctor of Divinity

degree by Highland College in May 1954. By the time of the synod meeting in Greenville, North Carolina, disagreement with Dr. Schaeffer and his position became clear. The Schaeffers didn't know whether they could return to the mission field or not. Battle lines were drawn, but not just over the Schaeffers. The denomination did split a year later, in 1955. The year 1955 marked the founding of Covenant College, Covenant Seminary, The Evangelical Presbyterian Church, and the Schaeffers' L'Abri Fellowship in Switzerland. Many people from L'Abri would later be sent to study at both Covenant College and Covenant Seminary, with some to return as Members and Workers in L'Abri. Some L'Abri workers have also attended Westminster Theological Seminary.

The Schaeffers prayed for money for passage to return to their work, and their prayers were answered. They returned to their mission field in Switzerland, but without the express blessing of their mission board. Some people were angry with them, because they thought Dr. Schaeffer was trying to take over the leadership of the denomination. Rather than try to take over the leadership of a denomination or found a new church, however, Fran and Edith chose to bury themselves in a tiny village in Switzerland, to seek and to do the Lord's work prayerfully and in the Lord's way, to see what fruit he might bring forth from the tiny grains of wheat of this one family. Later Dr. Schaeffer was to marvel at how much had been accomplished that never could have been done if he had stayed to fight battles within the denomination.

The result of Fran's walk in the hayloft of Chalet Bijou really did mark the turning point in his ministry. From the time of that walk in 1951, God began leading the

Schaeffers both through the teaching of his Word *and* experientially. Through specific answers to prayer, they began L'Abri as a faith ministry in 1955. With the five talks he gave in America on furlough, later expanded into the book *True Spirituality,* he began to insist, in a way that many were not yet ready to hear, that both reformation and revival were needed in the church. He said there must be a return to the sound teaching of the Bible (reformation) *and* a practice of that teaching under the power of the Holy Spirit (revival).

After the Schaeffers' return to Switzerland, their mission board acted upon Fran's emphasis of "the need of cleansing on the part of Christians, and of being dependent upon the Lord's strength and the power of the Holy Spirit, and of standing for truth with love."[7] The Schaeffers received a letter from the board, announcing that their salary would be cut by $100 per month. Furthermore, letters began to be sent to their supporting churches, expressing opposition to Schaeffer's teaching and work. Even Christian groups in other countries, with whom the Schaeffers had been working for several years, were receiving letters warning them of the Schaeffers' influence.

How could they survive and what would they do in a foreign country far from home, with virtually no funds to stay and no funds to leave, with their material supply lines being severed in salary cuts, and with dire warnings about them being sent to those who knew and cared for them?

1. *The Tapestry,* p. 315.
2. *True Spirituality,* in *The Complete Works,* Volume Three, Book Two, p. 346.
3. Ibid., p. 223.
4. *The Tapestry,* p. 350.
5. Ibid., p. 356.
6. Ibid., p. 388
7. Ibid., p. 394.

5
WALKING IN TRUTH

When Francis and Edith Schaeffer began L'Abri, they did not take a leap in the dark. For much of their ministry, and especially in the early years of the 1950s, they had been learning to walk in faith and truth one step at a time. They had prayed for a place to live while on furlough, and God had given them an immediate answer. They had prayed for money to return to Switzerland, and the money was provided in answer to prayer. A whole series of God's specific answers to prayer preceded their beginning of L'Abri. When the Scriptures also encouraged them in this ministry, they began L'Abri with good and sufficient reasons to think that this was God's will for their lives, and that he would be faithful in meeting all of their real needs for ministry. No leap in the dark was involved, but certainly a very exciting step of faith in totally relying upon God.

In January of 1955, Edith was reading from Isaiah as a part of her daily reading and time of prayer. When she came to Isaiah 2:2, 3 (RSV), she read: "It shall come to pass in the latter days that the mountain of the house of the Lord shall be established as the highest of the mountains, and shall be raised above the hills; and all the nations shall flow to it, and many peoples shall come and say: 'Come, let us go up to the mountain of the Lord, to the house of the God of Jacob; that he may teach us his ways and that we may walk in his paths.' " She believed God was telling her that was his promise for a *L'Abri* in the mountains of Switzerland.

That very real promise, given in the context of her praying about L'Abri, sustained her and Dr. Schaeffer in the many and trying difficulties ahead. This type of answer to prayer in the reading of the Scriptures has greatly guided Edith and Fran and their work throughout the years. Prayer sustained them in their conflicts, and God answered prayer to support them in their daily walk. Real answers to prayer gave them courage to keep on in the midst of very real trials, as Edith relates in her books.

Edith writes this about prayer in *The Tapestry:*

> *Prayer is a moment-by-moment example of the reality of the validity of choice.* God Himself has given us this communication for a diversity of reasons. One is that our calling upon the Father in Jesus' name, and in the power of the Holy Spirit, is time after time a slap in Satan's face, that proves the victory of Christ's death to defeat the primary purpose of Satan's temptation and the resultant separation of Adam and Eve, human beings, people, from communication with God.[1]

In their discussions at L'Abri, and in their many group discussions over the years, Dr. Schaeffer and Edith insisted that organizations and personalities should not be discussed. This idea came from the really difficult times with others, which followed his talks on sanctification. After his furlough there were many misunderstandings and personality clashes over Dr. Schaeffer and his public stands. Letters flew back and forth across the Atlantic, as Dr. Schaeffer tried to clarify his positions on sanctification, faith, the work of the Holy Spirit, and man's freedom and responsibility. Later some evangelical leaders would call him a humanist or a rationalist, because he tried to "think with" sinners and appeal to their reason to convince them to accept with the empty hands of faith the finished work of Jesus Christ in their behalf. From battles such as these within the church and without, he wisely decided that talking about people and organizations, rather than about ideas, would not really be helpful.

The battle is really for truth against falsehood, and the people who came to L'Abri needed to learn how to analyze the ideas that organizations or people expressed, not just pigeonhole people into categories and escape responsibility for thinking by saying, "The Schaeffers think this person or that group is wrong." Understanding how ideas influence the choices we make and the lifestyle we choose is of more lasting value as we analyze the world we encounter. Organizations and personalities change; they come and go. We become what we think about, and what we do often relates to the way we think. Dr. Schaeffer did not offer easy outs to people who did not want to think. He believed that one of the most lasting effects of discussion and study should be the knowledge of how to think clearly and logically, and of how to discern right from wrong ideas and ways of thinking.

No ideas were off limits for discussions. Just as Dr. Schaeffer and his family were to help others from their understanding of God and reality as based upon the Bible, so they learned from the many people who came, as they discussed books of all types, music, the arts, philosophy, theology, science, ethics, politics, law, drug use, current events around the world, medicine, alternative lifestyles, and the different religions. All these discussions would lead people to see how Christianity is related to the whole of life, to all disciplines and endeavors. Christian faith was not to be compartmentalized and unrelated to life. Both new and old Christians were called to walk in truth at all times and in all places. They were taught to confront wrong ideas and actions with love for others and out of respect for a holy God. They were encouraged not to build a "safe house" in which to live, but to learn about the Christian faith and be open to others' views so as to help them become Christians. Dr. Schaeffer warned: "A world spirit has always existed from the fall of Satan and of Adam and Eve. The creature wants to be autonomous from the Creator. This world spirit takes on different forms in each decade. We can be infiltrated by that form of the world spirit that surrounds us."[2] He wanted to teach people how to recognize the form the world spirit was taking in their decade, so they could resist and help others resist its infiltration.

The first four members of L'Abri, making up the official board, were George H. Seville, George Exhenry (who had been converted in Champery and was willing to take the persecution which attended his being a Christian publicly), and Francis and Edith Schaeffer. The children were also a vital part, as the whole family shared in the work of L'Abri and as they prayerfully made the decision to begin L'Abri together.

It would be impossible to say everything that could be said about L'Abri. All that can be done here is to open a door to understanding Dr. Schaeffer and his work. However, there are certain key events and dates that should be briefly summarized.

As early as 1949 the Schaeffers had been talking to students of many different backgrounds about Christianity. Zoroastrians, Buddhists, Hindus, atheists, agnostics, liberal Christians, Roman Catholics, and others of various anti-Christian and Christian views had been coming to their door. These students were from all over the world: Haiti, Argentina, Canada, England, Scotland, America, and the Scandinavian countries.

The Schaeffers had been in a ministry with students for more than six years prior to L'Abri's founding as a faith ministry. This is to emphasize again that in their work they did not take "leaps in the dark" any more than Dr. Schaeffer taught that Christian faith was a "leap in the dark" or a "leap of faith." Many similar enterprises have failed on this very account: people have leaped into the dark or they have leaped into a work without any clear knowledge that the work is truly God's will for them. If L'Abri had taken leaps in the dark over the years, it would have hindered their witness to the fact that people become Christians for good and sufficient reasons; they do not take a blind leap of faith. The aim of L'Abri, from its founding to the present, has been to walk prayerfully after good and sufficient reasons have been given by God for the next step.

Perhaps some have begun works similar to L'Abri, being inspired by the L'Abri story, only to have them fail because they were not really inspired by God or according to his will. Sometimes, while helping people to face their failed endeavors, Dr. Schaeffer was careful to tell them that if we make a mistake and begin a conscious Christian endeavor that is not on the track God really prefers, still he is able to work with us on that track or help us get on another track.

From the time of Edith's answer to prayer about L'Abri, up to and even beyond its official founding in June of 1955, times were not easy. Satan attacked and buffeted them all along the way, but what Satan meant for evil God meant for good, and worked to their good. Had it not been for her promise from God in the context of the prophet Isaiah, Edith could have felt that the trying events were designed by God to move them *from* Switzerland; instead, she saw them as part of the spiritual warfare in which they were deeply involved.

On February 14, 1955, Fran and Edith were officially notified that they had to leave Switzerland. They had had a "religious influence" in Champery; some people, like George Exhenry, had turned from trusting in their works to trusting in Christ for salvation. The Schaeffers were forbidden to return to Champery for two years. At the very time that things were beginning to break apart in their mission work, and with the denomination seeking to make things difficult, to say the least, they lost their home in Switzerland by an uncharacteristic government edict.

However, with remarkable answers to prayer, they were able to purchase Chalet les Mélèzes in the village of Huémoz, the Canton of Vaud. Mélèzes was named after the beautiful *mélèzes* or larch trees that grew between the chalet and the road. The Lord miraculously provided all the money they needed to make the down payment by the very day it was due. They had only three dollars left over after its purchase. This remarkable answer to prayer regarding their home in Switzerland, in the mountains for L'Abri, gave the Schaeffers the courage to write their mission board and resign. They had been enabled by God to move to Huémoz by April 1, the deadline set by the government; they had purchased their home by May 30, the deadline set by the home's owners.

L'Abri began in a very real way with Priscilla on the weekend of May 6, 1955. She brought home from college a girl who had many questions, and so began the flow of people. L'Abri came to be a spiritual "shelter" for people with real and honest questions. God's hand was so obviously in the work that Dr. Schaeffer courageously wrote his mission board on June 5 and resigned. He asked that all salary be cut off immediately, and he told of the beginning of L'Abri Fellowship. The Schaeffers had had the reality of the existence of God demonstrated to them in real ways up to that point, and L'Abri was begun simply from a desire "to demonstrate the existence of God by our lives and our work."[3]

They were successful because they began L'Abri with careful thought and prayer. They set out with a clearly defined purpose and goals. These goals were consistent with the teaching of Scripture. They did not develop a false pride in themselves or their work, but emphasized God's grace, for which they were thankful. They did not cease to rely upon careful thought, prayer, and the power of the Holy Spirit. They remained faithful in following God's inerrant Word to the best of their ability. They did not become authoritarian in their relationships, and they made changes in proven procedures slowly and prayerfully. They did not try to "hang on" to people or workers, but encouraged people to seek the Lord's will for their own lives and go where they felt he was leading them. Dr. Schaeffer often said, "I will not be the Holy Spirit for anybody." Every person was respected for his own creative talents and individuality; therefore, as the work grew, each L'Abri branch became an expression of each leader's own creativity. They were not restricted to a preset form. Within the bounds of Scripture, great freedom was encouraged. For these reasons, among others, they did not develop any of the characteristics we apply to the cults today. Any evaluation of their work should not be centered on whether or not they did things the way you or I would have done them, but upon whether or not they achieved goals that were substantially consistent with biblical teaching.

The purpose of L'Abri was "to show forth by demonstration, in our life and work, the existence of God."[4] If we ask, did they do this, the answer is yes. But they also set goals to achieve this purpose in specific ways; they would pray in four different areas. First, rather than appealing for money, they would pray for God to meet their material needs. Second, they would pray for God to send the people he wanted to L'Abri, and keep all others away. Third, they would pray for God's leading every day, rather than planning the work themselves. Fourth, they would pray for God to send the people he wanted to join them in the work.

They wanted to live in close contact with the supernatural world moment by moment, as though they had died, gone to heaven, and returned to tell others and show others that there really is a God who is there. They wanted to show that God would lead his people moment by moment, if they would live on the basis of faith in him moment by moment. As times have changed, their purpose has not changed, but as L'Abri has grown they look more and more to the leading of the Holy Spirit in making group decisions that affect the whole work.

At the beginning, Dr. George H. Seville became their

home secretary, and his wife mailed out Edith's family letter about their work to all who were interested. The Sevilles prayed for the Lord to meet all of L'Abri's needs, from the example they had learned from Hudson Taylor and the China Inland Mission. They prayed for the Lord to send the people of his choice to the work, both people with questions as well as workers, helpers, and students.

By November 1955, Dr. Schaeffer was heavily involved with the American GI's who were coming to L'Abri. He was traveling to the University of Lausanne where he met existentialists, humanists, Roman Catholics, liberal Protestants, and many others of a wide variety of philosophical and theological ideas.

By 1957, he was teaching medical and university students in Basel, and in the winter so many were coming to Huémoz that they needed to rent Chalet Beau Site for all that came.

In 1958 they began a work in London that later became English L'Abri. And during Christmas break of 1958, students came to Swiss L'Abri from Cambridge, Oxford, and St. Andrews Universities. One of those who came was Ranald Macaulay. He became one of the first students at Farel House (the study center) at L'Abri. Later, he and Susan Schaeffer Macaulay would spend twenty years of ministry in English L'Abri before moving to Huémoz and becoming directors of L'Abri internationally, following Dr. Schaeffer's death. An accomplished author, Susan has written books from her father's perspective, including *Something Beautiful from God, How to Be Your Own Selfish Pig,* and *For the Children's Sake.*

About the same time that L'Abri was being founded, Chalet les Sapins was being used by a vegetarian Hindu cult. Much prayer was made concerning the situation and for the people who were being misled by the ideas being taught there. Finally the owner died; having turned from the Light all around her, she died with great fears and insecurity. Chalet les Sapins was made a part of L'Abri in the mid 1960s.

By the late 1950s and early '60s, Fran began speaking all over the world. He spoke at all the major universities and colleges throughout England, Scotland, Wales, Ireland, and the United States. Having debated in college, he was a quick and able thinker who could present the case for Christianity reasonably and forcefully.

At Cambridge, he publicly debated a humanist in the midst of a humanist crowd. The crowd thought Fran had won the debate so handily that the humanist was embarrassed. Dr. Schaeffer then decided never to debate again. He would rather have discussions and try to win the person, than have debates to try to win the argument. In speaking of the debate many years later, he said, "Everyone knows that taking the Affirmative Side in a debate, and to speak first, is to take the weakest place. Before the debate, the humanist asked me what side I wanted, and I said, 'Oh, it doesn't matter, you choose.' The humanist decided that I should speak first and take the Affirmative Side. I hated to do it to him, but I simply got up and said briefly, 'I don't have enough faith to believe as the humanist, that everything just came from chance,' and then I sat down. The humanist then spent the rest of the time trying to get out of the box he was in, and he was actually booed by the humanist crowd. I had told all of the Christians to stay away."

Years later, Dr. Schaeffer was to have a public discussion with Bishop James Pike, and after the discussion,

Pike wanted to visit with him again. In that later visit, Bishop Pike told him that after he had become a Christian, he went to seminary (a prominent liberal seminary in New York City), and there they had robbed him of his faith and left him with only "a handful of pebbles." Dr. Schaeffer had learned how to discuss and not lose the person, even though the person might still refuse to be won to Christ.

One of the most exciting things about his work with students and answering their questions was seeing how people from all different walks of life were able to see the reality and the truth of the Christian answers. This is not to say that L'Abri was simply an intellectual discussion group. Many hippies came with their drug problems, with their minds swimming in clouds of unreality. These people required special care, but many got their thinking cleared up again, and then they accepted Christ as their personal Savior. Some came from the Christian counter-culture; these believed in Jesus, but their Jesus had no biblical content, a dangerous form of self-delusion. Some came saying they had been saved by Jesus, "but I don't believe in God." They too needed the teaching of L'Abri. In every case, Dr. Schaeffer aimed at speaking the truth and demonstrating the truth by his life.

This is not to say that Dr. Schaeffer was immediately successful with every student. In the late 1950s, one student from an English university dismissed Dr. Schaeffer's concerns as "mere intellectualism." Ten years later, on the mission field in Africa, he was struggling for answers to the questions he was being asked. And then Dr. Schaeffer's first books came into his hands. What he had dismissed as "intellectualism" ten years before became the solution to his dilemmas on the mission field of Africa. Born from the mission field in Switzerland, Dr. Schaeffer's work was never "ivory tower theology," but a practical guide for helping thinking people from all over the world become Christians and live a consistent Christian life.

Dr. Schaeffer kept himself open to the leading of God in all circumstances. It became obvious that God wanted him to reach out beyond selected college campuses and the little village of Huémoz to include as many people as possible in gatherings for teaching, with questions and answers. Dr. Schaeffer did not speak and run when he spoke publicly, but he opened himself to the challenges of other minds, those hostile to him or to Christianity, as well as to those who were sympathetic. He was motivated to open himself up to the strict questioning of his ideas, because he felt this was the most compassionate, caring, and nonmechanical way to do real evangelism. He also knew that the Bible and the God he represented could stand up very well in the public forum.

For all of these reasons, and others, the first of many L'Abri Conferences was held at the Ashburnham Conference grounds in England in the spring of 1968. Here 450 people from all walks of life—clergy, students, professors, professionals, laborers, and laypeople—came together for fellowship and discussion. With so many people needing to know what L'Abri was teaching, but with so many not being able to go to L'Abri, and with so many people wanting to bring "someone who really needs to hear this" to Dr. Schaeffer, the conferences were really the most loving thing that they could do next under the leading of God.

To enable Fran to meet the crushing demands of hundreds of people coming to Huémoz, of the heavy counseling of people with drug-related problems, of the need to write, of the need to speak outside of L'Abri, Miss Sheila Bird, "Birdie," a trained clinical psychologist, joined the Schaeffers in 1968. This time was also one of major challenge, as the hippies who came to L'Abri had no concern or compassion for the tiny and very conservative village of Huémoz. After a number of problems, the people of the village and L'Abri came to a mutual recognition of the needs of the young people as well as the needs of the village. When the Schaeffers moved to Chalet Chardonet in Chesieres, a thirty-minute hike up the hill from Huémoz, and after Dr. Schaeffer began his extended speaking tours from their new home, fewer students seemed to inundate Huémoz. Now they could learn from Dr. Schaeffer in person and from his books, without needing to travel all the way to Switzerland.

To understand him fully, we must realize that Dr. Schaeffer never sat around "trying to think up 'new theories' " or "theologizing" or "arguing for the sake of arguing" or trying to find "possible answers to possible questions." Instead, he received his training on the front lines of the spiritual battlefield, talking to real people with real questions, from all walks of life. He discovered from his deep involvement with individual human beings, and not just the human race in general, that most people were suffering from the same basic questions and the same basic problems. For these reasons, his books have had an almost immediate appeal all over the world, with people from a variety of cultures and backgrounds, and especially with thinking non-Christians.

Dr. Schaeffer did not thrust himself forward or try to be in the forefront of anything. If he was at the forefront as an evangelist to intellectuals or as a Protestant advocate of the pro-life cause, it was because God had "extruded him" (one of his favorite phrases when describing how people should look at their developing leadership roles) into that place of prominence at that time.

Dr. Schaeffer really buried himself in Switzerland, and he was willing to remain unknown in a small chalet, praying for the Lord to send the people of his choice for him to help. He really didn't want to administer a large and growing work in Huémoz or around the world, and that was not to be his final calling. God gave Dr. Schaeffer his own heart for his people around the world who could not go to that little chalet in Switzerland for help. And then God sent the leadership that was needed to administer a growing work.

Dr. Schaeffer's first books were published because reprints of his talks were soon demanded by those who had heard him and wanted others to hear too. His talks to American college students in 1965 became *The God Who Is There.* Hodder and Stoughton in England accepted this book in the spring of 1967, and it was published in 1968. *Escape from Reason* was published shortly thereafter, and then *Death in the City.* He got letters from everywhere on his first two books, even from the president of Senegal.

Radio talks began in December 1971 through the Trans-World Radio Station in Monte Carlo. These broadcasts reached all over Europe, behind the Iron Curtain, into the Near East and North Africa. Recorded in a tiny office now used by John Sandri (the husband of Priscilla), the talks brought more people to L'Abri, and some of the talks became books. The books enabled people to share his ideas in ways that could not have been possible otherwise. Today, a group of twenty-five wives of U.S. Congressmen meet every Friday morning to study systematically his books and Edith's. His twenty-three books have sold in the millions, and have been translated into at least twenty-four languages. When the family was moving to Rochester, they were amazed to pack at least 126 first editions of his works.

He was actively involved in formal theological education by becoming a visiting lecturer at Covenant Theological Seminary in St. Louis and at the Theological Academy in Basel, Switzerland. These times of lecturing away from home gave people who could not study for a prolonged time at Farel House in Huémoz the opportunity to think deeply and discuss openly with him how they could apply the gospel of Jesus Christ to the whole of life.

Dr. Schaeffer was welcomed not only at evangelical colleges, but also at most of the major Ivy League universities in America. In 1968 he spoke at Harvard. In 1972 he spoke at Princeton, and in 1973 he spoke at Yale. It was unusual to have large crowds worship in the Princeton University chapel on Sundays, but when he spoke, the 2,500-seat sanctuary was packed. Later, some of the university students went to the Princeton Seminary bookstore for books on apologetics (the rational defense of the Christian faith), but few were available. There was a real need for his books and lectures!

In addition to these American universities, he lectured at Helsinki University, Lund (Sweden) University, the Chinese University, Hong Kong University, and the University of Malaya. And on June 12, 1971, he was awarded the honorary Doctor of Letters degree from Gordon College. He also spoke to various groups in Washington, D.C., to White House workers in the Ford, Carter, and Reagan administrations, to members of Congress and their families, and to other government workers. For the last fifteen years of his ministry, he always had an open door for ministry among U.S. government leaders.

There was a reason for his wide influence in government and university circles. He took a rational, practical, prayerful, and compassionate approach to the biblical Christian faith. The rational approach was convincing to those who had to live on the cutting edge of human life. While he was answering people's questions, he was also praying for those who had to have answers for reality, who needed a foundation for making the right decisions—decisions that would affect millions of people in government, education, and business. Dr. Schaeffer understood modern man and the foundations of his ideas and actions. He did not to appeal to people's selfishness or self-interest by telling them to accept Christ for all that he could do for them. He presented Christianity as *the only viable option that is true to reality,* and then he demanded that people live on the basis of Christian truth.

1. *The Tapestry,* p. 420.
2. Personal communication with the author.
3. *The Tapestry,* p. 432.
4. Edith Schaeffer, *L'Abri* (Wheaton: Tyndale House, 1969), pp. 15-16.

6
SPEAKING THE TRUTH IN LOVE

IN 1974 Dr. Schaeffer addressed the Lausanne Congress on World Evangelization, declaring that the church today must emphasize Christian holiness, purity of life, and purity of doctrine. Christians must realize the reality of God and the supernatural in the midst of this present life, and this cannot be forgotten as they try to do evangelism. "Evangelism that does not lead to purity of life and purity of doctrine is just as faulty and incomplete as an orthodoxy which does not lead to a concern for, and communication with, the lost."[1]

His talk at the Congress was published as *Two Contents, Two Realities.* Dr. Schaeffer was prophetic. Ten years before he wrote *The Great Evangelical Disaster,* he warned: "Almost certainly if we have a latitudinarianism in religious cooperation, the next generation will have a latitudinarianism in doctrine, *and especially a weakness toward the Bible."*[2]

The inerrancy of Scripture is the watershed issue for Bible-believing churches. Once the inerrancy of Scripture is given up, disastrous consequences will follow as one by one the essential Christian doctrines will be questioned and begin to fall. But if the conservative and evangelical churches would return to their historic and *really biblical* position on the authority and the inerrancy of Scripture, Dr. Schaeffer believed, with the Apostle Paul:

> Then we will no longer be infants, tossed back and forth by the waves, and blown here and there by every wind of teaching and by the cunning and craftiness of men in their deceitful scheming. Instead, *speaking the truth in love,* we will in all things grow up into him who is the Head, that is, Christ. From him the whole body, joined and held together by every supporting ligament, grows and builds itself up in love, as each part does its work. So I tell you this, and insist on it in the Lord, that you must no longer live as the Gentiles do, in the futility of their thinking. (Ephesians 4:14-17)

Dr. Schaeffer emphasized that concern for the purity of the church should not lead to the hatred, bitterness, and unloveliness that had characterized his experiences in the '30s, '40s, and '50s. He pleaded for truth. But as he always endeavored to speak the truth in love, he called for others to make love their aim as they spoke for the truth of God. This cannot be done in the flesh, but only in the power of the indwelling Holy Spirit; therefore, Dr. Schaeffer built his life and work on prayer, in a moment by moment communication with God, and he insisted that we do the same.

Often he would discuss the problems of Bible-believing Christians who stayed in the liberal denominations in hopes of bearing their witness, and the Bible-believing Christians who felt called to leave. He emphasized the they should not separate from one another, but they should support one another in truth and love of the Lord. His advice to those struggling about what to do included, "I cannot be the Holy Spirit for anyone. You must pray about these things and seek the Lord's leading. The Holy Spirit can call some to stay in, and he can call others to come out." On the other hand, he also added, "I know for myself that I could never have accomplished what I have for the Lord if I had stayed in and had tried to fight the battles from the inside."

He noted that in recent history, only one mainline denomination had fought the battle for the Bible in their church and won against the liberals. In some other denominations, the battle had not yet been decided. His observations led him to warn that when the bureaucracy and the seminaries have been captured by the liberals the battle is lost. The liberals have always tended to infiltrate, subvert, and overtake institutions from the inside. They have never created a major theological institution, with perhaps the exception of the World Council of Churches.

To help Christians learn that in the battles we face, we must always speak the truth in love, he wrote *The Church before the Watching World.* He was literally moved to tears when he learned that his teachings in that book had helped many Bible-believing Christians maintain fellowship one with another, although they might be in different churches. Dr. Schaeffer believed that if we hold to the essentials of the Christian faith, then we have a large circle of people who also hold to the essentials, with whom we can cooperate and have fellowship, even though they may be in churches of other denominations. Still, he was to insist strongly that those who stay in the liberal denominations cannot accommodate the liberals, but must continue to confront them with love in all areas of truth in practice and doctrine.

In 1974 Dr. Schaeffer also began to work with his son Franky on a new project—a project that marked a turning point in the lives of many people. They began work on the book and film series, *How Should We Then Live?* Filmed in Germany, Switzerland, France, Italy, England, Holland, Belgium, and the United States, the filming took six months to complete. It has been translated into German, Spanish, and Japanese. The book and film were written as a response to Kenneth Clark's book *Civilisation.* Clark was an atheist, though he seemed to believe that Eastern religious thought was the pinnacle of man's religious reaching for spiritual enlightenment. His book took a definite anti-Christian stance, and his film series from the book was aired widely over public television.

Dr. Schaeffer's book and film were the Christian response to Clark and others who teach that Christianity is the enemy of intellectual endeavors and achievements. As Dr. Schaeffer's work swept over the whole of Western intellectual life and thought, many realized for the first time that Christianity *did* have the intellectual answers to the philosophical questions—questions that had been raised on the university level, but left unanswered in liberal seminaries. As one pastor commented, after seeing the series, "Now all the pieces fit together! My Christian faith used to be just a jumble of puzzle pieces, of truths that didn't fit together with the world as it is. For the first time I can see the beautiful picture of Christian truth. The puzzle has been put together; I see how everything fits!"

How Should We Then Live? demonstrated beautifully what Dr. Schaeffer struggled with in all of his books: "To make a reality day by day of the lordship of Christ in the whole of life, in the area of culture as well as all else . . . to broaden the reality of honestly exhibiting the lordship of Christ in regard to social issues and political life, law, medicine (human life), and government."[3] For this reason, and because of the scope of his works, *The Complete Works of Francis A. Schaeffer* is subtitled *A Christian Worldview.*

Completely revised, with new appendices added in 1982, Schaeffer's *Complete Works* show us not only the full scope of his learning but also why he was able to give to the world a new respect for the names "fundamentalist" or "evangelical." By the time *The Complete Works* was completed, however, evangelicalism's teachings were in such disarray and some of them so antibiblical that he chose to call himself a "Bible-believing Christian" and talk about a standing for "Bible-believing Christianity."

The intellectual integrity of Bible-believing Christianity really began to make an impact upon the masses and sweep across the American continent when the first seminar for the film series was held in January 1977, with 5,600 people attending. That was the same year both Hans Rookmaaker and Edith's father, George Seville, died. Also, the chapel in Huémoz was burned. It appeared that Satan was attacking from many sides. But what Satan meant for evil, God obviously could turn for good. Edith has said, "Satan so often attacks in ways which the Lord turns into something powerful in counterattack."[4] Satan did not want *How Should We Then Live?* to have an impact, but with every attack from

Satan the Schaeffers and L'Abri demonstrated the truth of their teachings in life and gave their teachings even more credibility.

Many answers to prayer sustained the Schaeffers and L'Abri during very difficult times, and the book and the film series have had a remarkable effect upon Western culture and the Christian leaders in various governments around the world. *How Should We Then Live?* was a major attempt to warn the churches and Western governments of coming dangers from a historical perspective, as Dr. Schaeffer became one of the "watchmen who saw the sword coming and blew the trumpet" (see Ezekiel 33:1-19). He did so by using the best medium that he could use, a contemporary film.

Just as Dr. Schaeffer was pausing to rest a bit after writing the book, doing the film, and completing the tour, Franky was inspired to do yet another film project, after hearing Dr. C. Everett Koop speak at a series of meetings at Swiss L'Abri. Long conversation with Dr. Koop, into the wee hours of the morning, convinced Franky, who then convinced his father that they should write a book and do a film with Dr. Koop that would eventually become *Whatever Happened to the Human Race?* This film on abortion, infanticide, and euthanasia rocked the Western world and brought to Dr. Schaeffer vehement protests and even threats on his life, as well as praise—eventually, praise from President Ronald Reagan and the English Parliament for awakening the Protestant conscience to the central moral issue of our time. Dr. Schaeffer brought a new biblical intellectual integrity to Christian social involvement.

Many viewers felt incredulous as the film spoke of the possibility of infanticide in the future. But at the film seminars, time after time, clergy and medical people told of children being starved to death in nearby hospitals in recent years. Some were starved simply because their handicap and need for surgery were an inconvenience to the parents and/or the doctors concerned. Regarding the treatment of the elderly, some doctors have said bluntly, "Society has a concern here," as they have pressured families to decide to terminate their feeding.

The film series raised issues that Christians and others needed to be discussing. Some evangelical churches didn't want to disrupt their evangelism programs or "rock their boats," and so they tried to ignore the issues that Dr. Schaeffer and Dr. C. Everett Koop, now U.S. Surgeon General, were making. Many others, however, did listen. Perhaps millions more will listen to the call to save lives and to change laws in those countries that allow the civil rights of unborn children to be violated by their mothers who have abortions and by doctors who murder children for hire. Abortion in America is a multimillion-dollar business, with 476 abortions being performed for every 1,000 live births. Powerful forces are at work to continue these brutal murders. Many abortion advocates even argue that to preserve the human race we need to kill as many of our unborn children as possible. *Whatever Happened to the Human Race!*

During this same year, 1977—the year Rookmaaker had died, the year she lost her father at 101, when satanic attacks seemed to be at their height and a new project to save human life had begun—Edith Schaeffer wrote the book *Affliction*. The book was finished by October 2, 1977. One year later the Schaeffers were flying to Rochester to Mayo Clinic, where they would hear that Dr. Schaeffer had lymphoma. Some doctors felt he had only from six weeks to six months to live. Edith believes that her book *Affliction* was given to them as well as to others, by the Lord, to help sustain them over the years ahead. Many pastors and counselors have found in her book real answers for afflicted, sick, and dying people. *Affliction* gave needed answers from a whole, rather than a fragmented, Christian perspective. It has been a blessed gift to many who have needed to read a biblical interpretation for their suffering.

The filming for *Whatever Happened to the Human Race?* was begun in August, and by October of 1978, after the final day of filming, preparations were being made to get Dr. Schaeffer to the hospital. He had lost more than twenty-five pounds, was exhausted, and found breathing difficult. On September 18, 1978, they had filmed the scenes on the shore of Galilee about the risen Christ, footage that was shown at Dr. Schaeffer's funeral. Of that fifth episode of the film Dr. Schaeffer said, "It is the best presentation of the gospel I have ever been able to make." It was fitting that he could present his own final statement about the Christian hope through that film episode at his funeral.

On Tuesday, October 10, 1978, they were met at the Rochester airport by their friends Dr. Victor Wahby and Dr. Carl Morlock. Dr. Robert M. Pettit began treatment for lymphoma on October 17th. They had found a tumor the size of a football.

Dr. Schaeffer's cancer went into remission at least twice in answer to prayer and in response to the excellent medical treatment he received. He saw no inconsistency between receiving medical attention, a gift from God as a part of the battle in this fallen world, and faith in God to bring healing. Medicine and faithful prayer go together. God empowered Dr. Schaeffer to live five more years, because he had more work for Dr. Schaeffer to do.

Dr. Schaeffer never gave up. He remarked: "I have felt the power and the authority of God in my life over these past five years. By God's grace, I have been able to do more in these last five years than in all the years before I had cancer." Dr. Schaeffer was needed as a Christian public figure to demonstrate that no matter what the battle, we are to "keep on, keep on," and never give up. He insisted that in fighting an illness, we are not fighting God or God's will for our lives. There is no inconsistency between taking medicine and praying for healing. Taking medicine is not a sign of lack of faith. And being ill is not a sign of lack of faith either.

The Word of God sustained his faith, and one of the Scriptures that encouraged him most was Psalm 84, verses 5-7:

> Blessed are those whose strength is in you, who have set their hearts on pilgrimage. As they pass through the Valley of Baca [Valley of Weeping], they make it a place of springs; the autumn rains also cover it with pools. They go from strength to strength till each appears before God in Zion.

Dr. Schaeffer went "from strength to strength" several times during his illness, and when he went to meet the Lord at the end of his faithful pilgrimage (and at the end of his personally giving to people springs of "living water" to drink), he went on "from strength to strength."

We should be inspired when we think of what Dr. Schaeffer did for the world while he was fighting against cancer and for his own life.

He continued to walk three miles a day, as often as he was able. The strong heart he had acquired from his many hikes in the Alps, from chopping wood for the wood stoves, and from his gardening and landscaping work outdoors, had prepared him physically to withstand the damaging effect of chemotherapy as it attacked his good cells as well as the bad. He looked upon many of his walks as quiet times to pray and be with the Lord in the beautiful world God had made.

By January 1979, in Rochester, he began to speak to various groups of doctors and hospital chaplains. He showed the complete series of *How Should We Then Live?* to a full auditorium at the John Marshall High School in Rochester. After having chemotherapy in the morning, he answered questions on almost every subject in the evening. Many hearers were convinced of the sufficiency of the Bible's answers to the questions life poses.

Even during the early months of his treatments, people continued to come into his home with questions as they sought to find the reality of the Christian faith. Some came seeking the faith that had been stolen from them by their liberal churches. Often, as he would sit in a waiting room at Mayo Clinic, people would see him and come and ask, "Are you Dr. Schaeffer?" He would say "Yes, I am." They would express warm appreciation for his books and films, or ask deep and perplexing questions as he waited to see the doctors or take treatment. He made himself accessible to people, and he never stopped praying every day, "Lord, send the people of *your* choice."

At one point a young girl was struggling to find freedom from a local cult. She wrote a letter to Dr. Schaeffer. He called and talked to her on the phone. His compassion for her and the time he gave in the very midst of his own illness saved her faith and gave her the strength to make the final break from the cult. Since then his books and films have inspired her own lay ministry.

Dr. Schaeffer was accessible to almost everyone at all times, but that does not mean that it was easy for him. He suffered quietly from his illness as he tried to help others with whatever problems they might have. He would often call on patients in the hospitals in Rochester, when people would express a need of whatever sort. In a speech to the chaplains of Mayo Clinic at this time, he told them he was glad he had something to say in the midst of the absurdity of cancer and the other horrible diseases people suffer. He said, "I can go talk to patients and tell them, 'God hates your cancer. God *hates* your cancer.' And I am encouraged when I remember that at the tomb of Lazarus 'Jesus wept,' and he could weep and be angry at death, even though he was God. He could be angry at death, and not be angry at himself as the Creator."

Dr. Schaeffer knew this is a fallen world, and he had something to say because his faith was firmly grounded on the content of the Bible. He could help people to act in faith upon the total unified Christian teaching of God's Word. He could remind people that we live in a supernatural universe—that ever since the rebellion of man we face a battle. This battle is in the seen as well as in the unseen world. And so he would encourage people to be contented before God and yet fight the battle against their disease.

Throughout his own long suffering, Dr. Schaeffer manifested contentment before God. He maintained a quiet disposition and gave thanks to God for his love to him. His trust in his heavenly Father never failed or faltered. He would ask his Father, "What do you want me to learn from this?" A special hospital ministry, based upon the Christian teaching of the Bible, is still carried on by L'Abri in Rochester today.

In the summer of 1979, the first of two Rochester L'Abri Conferences was held. Almost two thousand people attended, coming from forty-seven states. Dr. Schaeffer insisted during the planning meetings that the advertising must be out of *compassion*. After some of their past conferences, many hurting people had written, "If only we had known!" For many people in Rochester, and for others attending a conference for the first time, the various members of L'Abri who spoke showed the depth of knowledge and understanding that the leaders in every branch of L'Abri possess. In between their lectures they all gave themselves totally to answering the questions brought by many troubled people. They didn't even have time to hear one another speak!

Dr. Schaeffer's motive was to help as many hurting people as he could, with the short time that he had left. He did not seek glory or honor for himself. He was humble before the Lord, and the Lord raised him up and honored him. When someone praised him, he would say simply "Well, I am grateful." He lived to honor God and to lead people to accept Jesus Christ as their Savior, making him the Lord of all life. He strove to help all people be of help to others on the basis of the truth of the Scripture.

In September 1979, the seminars for *Whatever Happened to the Human Race?* began in Philadelphia, traveling from East to West. Later, Minnesota Citizens Concerned for Life and other such groups would buy the film and make it available to be shown for pro-life causes around the country. On January 22, 1981, Minnesota Governor Al Quie honored Dr. Schaeffer for his work in the pro-life movement, at a special dinner at the governor's mansion in St. Paul.

The October before he died, on Wednesday afternoon, October 26, 1983, Dr. Schaeffer led a silent, dignified march of six people in front of the Methodist Hospital in Rochester, Minnesota, to protest against the hospital and some of the Mayo Clinic doctors for performing abortions at that hospital. He also wanted to show that a small group can still make a quiet and orderly statement for the lives of unborn children. Three men and three women dressed neatly in business suits carried six placards bearing a unified message: "This hospital is normally committed to saving human life; but abortion reverses this; abortion is the killing of a human life; abortion devaluates the unique value of all human life; it is the value of everyone's life which is involved; abortion is the killing of a human life." At the conclusion of the march, Dr. Schaeffer told reporters what he had said so often: "What they ought to realize is that they are schizophrenic. A policy of healing and the practice of abortion on demand are contradictory."[5] Some who passed the hospital that day hadn't even known that the clinic doctors performed abortions there!

With *How Should We Then Live?* Dr. Schaeffer demonstrated the necessity of the biblical Christian answers as the foundation for human life, and he showed the intellectual substance of biblical Christian faith when compared to other ideas. *Whatever Happened to the Human Race?* emphasized the necessity of moral absolutes based upon the Bible and carried his concern to the next logical step: to social action based upon these moral absolutes and the principles that could be derived from them.

God kept Dr. Schaeffer alive during twenty strenuous seminars for *Whatever Happened to the Human Race?* but by February 1980, the cancer was back in full force again. He did not stop, however; he went to the White House to talk with Christian leaders, and while he was in Washington he conducted another seminar of *Whatever Happened to the Human Race?* with other government leaders. This seminar, along with much other work by many people, has given intellectual and moral strength to those in Congress and in the White House who are in favor of protecting human beings of all ages.

Next, Dr. Schaeffer crossed the Atlantic for more seminars in England. Dr. Koop and an English doctor held discussions with him. These efforts almost single-handedly caused a radical change of opinion in much of England regarding the sanctity of human life. Later, Malcolm Muggeridge, Mother Teresa, and others would join Dr. Schaeffer at Hyde Park where fifty thousand people rallied to promote the sanctity of human life and then march to Trafalgar Square.

By 1979 L'Abri had moved its American headquarters to Rochester so Dr. Schaeffer would have a "work" to come to when he came for his medical treatments. Discussions were held on Monday nights in their home, and later they grew so large that they needed to meet in the Plummer House, a mansion built by the late Dr. Henry Plummer of Mayo Clinic and then given to the City of Rochester for such use. People from a great variety of intellectual backgrounds and interests, Christians as well as non-Christians, profited from these discussions. Many who came did not realize Dr. Schaeffer was often in the midst of chemotherapy treatments. Over and over again the doctors would tell him, "Now everyone gets *really* sick from this type of chemical," but over and over again his heavenly Father would surprise them at how well he did. He did have times of great tiredness, depression, intense pain, and other complications, but through it all God was gentle and compassionate.

On some occasions church groups from various denominations would travel to see him at his home in Rochester to ask advice on how they could fight the battle for truth within their denomination. At other times he would be asked to speak at a variety of denominational meetings. In a few cases he was the first person ever allowed to speak at a meeting, where the denomination required that the speaker had to be a member of that denomination.

As a Presbyterian minister, Dr. Schaeffer had his own distinctive, reformed view of the sacraments and other matters. But Baptists, Lutherans, and others knew that he would not get off into denominational distinctives and push these views in a public debate; rather, they knew that Dr. Schaeffer could be trusted to help them fight for the truth in the essential places where the battles needed to take place. For this reason, most Bible-believing churches welcomed him gladly as a speaker, and he had more requests to speak than he could possibly fulfill.

Dr. Schaeffer had the gift of fighting where the battle should take place and of keeping peace where there should be peace among Bible-believing Christians and their churches. When he edited his *Complete Works,* he made certain that it included biblical views that all Bible-believing Christians should agree upon, and for this reason his books have been used by a broad spectrum of Bible-believing Christians and different denominations. Once, a prominent Christian college asked him if it could establish a Francis A. Schaeffer Department of Philosophy in his honor. He turned down the honor out of humility and because he did not want to place something that might be a barrier to some between his work and any other Bible-believing denomination. He did not allow personal pride to blind him to the essentials!

Dr. Schaeffer could have quit after his seminars for *Whatever Happened to the Human Race?,* but the seminars only reinforced for him the necessity of continued fighting in two crucial areas. He would say, "How can I think of retiring at a time like this!" First, he began to fight harder for freedom of religion and freedom of speech in governments that suppressed the truth. He often wore a *Solidarity* button, to identify with the Polish people in their struggle against totalitarianism.

But the battle also needed to be fought in America, as religious ideas were being systematically shut out of the schools and other institutions. It was as though the United States and Russia had something in common; in neither country could a person acknowledge the existence of God in the schoolroom! Christians were being denied their first amendment rights of free speech and assembly, simply because they were Christians! We can be thankful that Dr. Schaeffer's battle cry was heard by many Christian leaders and churches, and Congress has now acted to restore to children *some* of the rights that the Supreme Court had denied them.

Second, in his last years, it brought him much weeping to have to fight for the truth and the authority of the Bible in the churches that claimed to be evangelical or conservative. Having lived through the liberal takeover of the churches in the early '30s, he understood far too well what many of the younger evangelicals were selling out in their eagerness to accommodate the new liberal forces. He knew how easily false ideas could infiltrate minds and churches. He had warned and probably saved the evangelical churches from Barthianism in the 1950s, but now there are many intelligent and courageous Christian leaders who will carry on his battle for the Bible and insist that the Scriptures be accepted as true in all that they affirm.

People needed to fight for their freedoms and also for the truth. But in writing the best-seller *A Christian Manifesto,* he wept for his Christian brothers and sisters in the Eastern bloc, people who had to pay a real price for their convictions. He prayed that some radicals would not take his ideas and twist them and use them in wrong ways in the name of Christ. Because of his work in this area, in 1983 he received the honorary Doctor of Laws Degree from Simon Greenleaf School of Law. Still, he wondered, "Will Christians in America stand up and fight for their freedoms, where there is really no price *as yet* to pay for doing so?"

Then, shortly before his death, he wrote *The Great Evangelical Disaster,* much of which he had to proofread from his hospital bed. One month before Dr. Schaeffer died, God gave him strength to complete a thirteen-seminar tour on his book. Those who knew him saw God give him supernatural strength to do his will the last six months of his life, as he had to get the message of *The Great Evangelical Disaster* into the churches and college campuses. He prayed that Christians, and especially pastors, would be willing to fight as well as speak in love for the truth of God's Word in their churches—no matter what the personal cost—for the sake of the truth and the next generation.

Dr. Schaeffer saw all these efforts as the practice of "true spirituality," and that is why he was particularly pleased with the reworking of *True Spirituality* in his *Complete Works.* This book really opens the door to an understanding of Dr. Schaeffer, the man. It was the book that really laid out the foundation for all of his subsequent work. Apparently none of his critics have seriously considered what he wrote in that book about the centrality of personal Christian experience based upon the objective truth of the Bible and the finished work of Christ on the cross, and then of the need to be involved in the whole of life on that basis.

By April 1984, Dr. Schaeffer was exhausted. He spent Easter Sunday in the cancer ward at St. Mary's Hospital, while doctors thought about possible treatments and fought for his life, trying to find just the right formula that might turn the tide once again. But Dr. Schaeffer could not remember when he had ever been so tired. He looked forward to living with Edith in their new home not far from the hospital and near the other L'Abri homes. He was intrigued about what work God would have him do now. But at the same time, he wanted to go to be with Jesus. On one occasion he said, "One of these days I am going to go to sleep and not wake up." He showed no fear. At other times, he reminded those nearby about the importance of spreading the Word of God, of upholding the truth of the Bible, of fighting for human life. He knew that Jesus had prepared a place for him, and sometimes he would pray for Jesus to take him home; yet he, like the Apostle Paul, wanted to stay.

During his last weeks in the hospital, Dr. Schaeffer wanted private time with his family. He had been so much in the public view all his life that he really wanted only Edith and the family to be at his side. He found comfort from his L'Abri workers and from the many cards and flowers that were sent him, but essentially, he wanted to be alone with his family or his doctors.

The doctors finally said that there was nothing else they could do. One option was to put him into an intensive care unit, where he could see his family only for brief times every few hours. Another option was simply to let him stay in his hospital room. The option they chose was to let him go home to be with his family among the familiar surroundings of the furnishings Edith had hurriedly brought from their old home in Switzerland, to provide a place of continuity in the midst of change. Edith told him gently, "We are traveling on different roads together, roads that neither of us has ever traveled before." He went to their new home knowing he had but a short time left with his wife and family. But he went home still fighting for his life. A few days before he died, Mayo Clinic doctors went to his home with one more dose of chemotherapy. He told them quietly, "Thank you for fighting."

Nurses who later attended him at home continually marveled at how much support his own family gave him in his illness. They had never seen such support from a family before; they saw Christian faith make a real difference. Even in one of their most difficult hours, the Schaeffers were still testifying to the substantial reality we can have with our heavenly Father through faith in Jesus Christ.

Dr. Schaeffer died early in the morning of May 15, 1984. He left quietly to be with the Lord, and the Lord encouraged his family with an appropriate reading that he knew they would read from *Daily Light,* the reading for that day. Debby brought it to the attention of the family, and it was read at his funeral in Rochester and again at a simple graveside service one year later to encourage his family and close friends to keep on. On a bright and beautiful day, May 20, 1984, as eight hundred people crowded the auditorium of the John Marshall High School, the site of his two L'Abri Conferences and other meetings, these words rang out:

He will wipe every tear from their eyes. There will be no more death or mourning or crying or pain, for the old order of things has passed away.

He will swallow up death forever. . . . The Sovereign Lord will wipe away the tears from all faces; he will remove the disgrace of his people from all the earth. The Lord has spoken. . . . No one living in Zion will say, "I am ill"; and the sins of those who dwell there will be forgiven. . . . The sound of weeping and of crying will be heard in it no more. . . . Sorrow and sighing will fly away.

I will ransom them from the power of the grave; I will redeem them from death. Where, O death, are your plagues? Where, O grave, is your destruction?—The last enemy to be destroyed is death. . . . Then the saying that is written will come true: "Death has been swallowed up in victory."

What is unseen is eternal.

God raised us up with Christ.

"Do not be afraid. . . . I am the living One." "Father, I want those you have given me to be with me where I am."

For we are members of his body. And he is the head of the body, the church; he is the beginning and the firstborn from among the dead. . . . You have been given fullness in Christ, who is the head over every power and authority.

Since the children have flesh and blood, he too shared in their humanity so that by his death he might destroy him who holds the power of death—that is, the devil—and free those who all their lives were held in slavery by their fear of death.

For the perishable must clothe itself with the imperishable, and the mortal with immortality. When the perishable has been clothed with the imperishable, the mortal with immortality, then the saying that is written will come true: "Death has been swallowed up in victory."[6]

Is the Bible just words? Are these particular words "only a positive statement in the midst of an absurd situation"? No! A thousand times, no! God is there! God has not been silent! God has spoken! When a Christian dies, there is an eternal difference; he knows that through Christ his sins are forgiven, and that he goes to a place he has prepared for him. When Christians who are left behind say "good-bye" to a loved one who they know will go to be with the Lord, the fact that God has spoken *truly* makes all the difference.

Regarding Dr. Schaeffer's journey to be with his great Friend, Edith wrote:

> It was 4 AM precisely that a soft last breath was taken. . . . and he was absent. That absence was so sharp and precise! Absent. Now I only observed the absence. I can vouch for the absence being precisely at 4 AM . . . as can Debby and Sue, and Shirley, the nurse (a L'Abri person from Canada). As for his presence with the Lord . . . I had to turn to my BIBLE to know that. I only know that a person is present with the Lord because the *Bible* tells us so. I did not have a mystical experience. I want to tell you here and now that the inerrant Bible became more important to me than ever before. I want to tell you very seriously and solemnly . . . the Bible is more precious than ever to me. My husband fought for truth and fought for the truth of the inspiration of the Bible—the inerrancy of the Bible—all the days that I knew him . . . through my 52 years of knowing him. But—never have I been more impressed with the wonder of having a trustworthy message from God, an unshakable word from God—than right then! I did not have to have, nor pretend to have, some mystical experience to prove that Fran had left to go somewhere . . . that he had gone TO the prepared place for him, and that he was indeed OK. I could know that by turning to my precious Bible, and to his precious Bible (and we each have had several), and read again that absent from the body is present with

the Lord . . . and that is far better. It is far better for the one who is thus present—but not for those left behind. God knows all about the pain of separation . . . and is preparing that separation will be over forever one future day. I also know that because the Bible tells me so. I feel very sorry for the people who have to be "hoping without any assurance" . . . because they *don't know* what portion of the Bible is myth and what portion might possibly be trusted. What fear must clutch their hearts as the face of their loved one suddenly turns to wax after the last breath announces the absence!![7]

1. *The Tapestry,* p. 575.

2. *Two Contents, Two Realities,* in *The Complete Works,* Volume Three, Book Four, p. 411.

3. *The Tapestry,* pp. 591, 592.

4. *L'Abri Family Letter,* December 29, 1973, by Edith Schaeffer.

5. *The Rochester Post-Bulletin,* October 27, 1983, p. 13.

6. *Daily Light on the Daily Path,* from The New International Version, The Zondervan Corporation, 1981.

7. *L'Abri Family Letter,* July 17, 1984, by Edith Schaeffer, p. 9.

FRANCIS A. SCHAEFFER IV

THE MESSAGE

IF YOU CONFESS WITH YOUR MOUTH, "JESUS IS LORD," AND BELIEVE IN YOUR HEART THAT GOD RAISED HIM FROM THE DEAD, YOU WILL BE SAVED. FOR IT IS WITH YOUR HEART THAT YOU BELIEVE AND ARE JUSTIFIED, AND IT IS WITH YOUR MOUTH THAT YOU CONFESS AND ARE SAVED. AS THE SCRIPTURE SAYS, "EVERYONE WHO TRUSTS IN HIM WILL NEVER BE PUT TO SHAME." FOR THERE IS NO DIFFERENCE BETWEEN JEW AND GENTILE— THE SAME LORD IS LORD OF ALL AND RICHLY BLESSES ALL WHO CALL ON HIM, FOR "EVERYONE WHO CALLS ON THE NAME OF THE LORD WILL BE SAVED."

HOW, THEN, CAN THEY CALL ON THE ONE THEY HAVE NOT BELIEVED IN? AND HOW CAN THEY BELIEVE IN THE ONE OF WHOM THEY HAVE NOT HEARD? AND HOW CAN THEY HEAR WITHOUT SOMEONE PREACHING TO THEM? AND HOW CAN THEY PREACH UNLESS THEY ARE SENT? AS IT IS WRITTEN, "HOW BEAUTIFUL ARE THE FEET OF THOSE WHO BRING GOOD NEWS!" ROMANS 10:9-15

7
HOW DO WE KNOW?

IS THERE TRUTH and falsehood? Is there right and wrong? Are some things absolutely true and right? Or is everything relative, just a matter of personal opinion and individual preference? Perhaps a simple illustration can help us answer these questions.

Let's assume that I am in a room with one hundred people, and I am holding a large silver coin high in the air. Let's further assume that there has just been a vote, and 60 percent of the people think that the coin is a liquid and 39 percent think it is a gas. Now, both groups cannot be right, because their answers are opposite. But we can readily see from the illustration that both groups could be wrong. Let's further suppose that the other 1 percent believes the coin is a solid, and that we have exhausted all of the possibilities.

We know that only one view can be right, and the other two must be wrong. Whether the coin is a solid, liquid, or gas is not just a matter of personal opinion. In this practical illustration we know that some things are absolutely right and some things are absolutely wrong. But how are we going to decide what the coin is? If we just take a majority vote, based upon the opinions of those present, we may still be wrong, and indeed in the case we are discussing, the majority is wrong. Even though 60 percent of the group believes that the large silver coin is a liquid, it has the physical properties of a solid.

What can we do then? What we should do in the situation is study some discoveries of science—perhaps read about liquids, gases, and solids in the encyclopedia, and then test the silver coin to see if it has the properties of any of those options. We could also pray to God and ask him to help us in our scientific study and investigation, to help us find the truth.

When we have discovered that the coin is really a solid, no matter what others may say it is, then we have to convince the other 99 percent of the group that we are right in calling the coin a solid. As a matter of fact, it is our obligation to convince the other side that the coin is a solid, because it is a matter of truth. Of course, this is easier if the whole group has been studying together or if we can lead the group in a thorough study of the matter, but sometimes the majority is not open to further investigation. This may not be an easy matter, because all sorts of prejudices might complicate the situation. Maybe some are too proud to admit that they were wrong, and maybe others *want* to believe, at least in theory, that everything is relative and that there is no absolute truth or right regarding anything.

In reality, we know that no one can live very long if he does not understand and act upon the difference between liquids, gases, and solids. People can't even eat and drink properly if they do not recognize the difference!

The principles we find in this illustration also apply to religions and to ideas about morality or philosophy. If 60 percent of those in my hypothetical room believe in Hinduism and 39 percent believe in Islam, both groups cannot be right, because their ideas are opposite, but both groups could be wrong. We know they cannot both be right because their ideas about who God is are radically different from the core of reality. Of course, in the area of different religions, the options are far more varied than three, but the principles for finding out which one is true and which ones are false are the same.

One religion, among all the many choices, is closer to reality than the others. To find which is true to reality, we can study the different religions, perhaps again use a good encyclopedia, read the books of the various religions, test what we read with the world as we know it to be, and then pray that God will lead us to find him in the appropriate way and adopt the appropriate beliefs about him. When we discover that the different religions contradict one another, especially in their views regarding the God who is there, we know that they cannot all be right. Indeed, some religions are out of touch with reality. When we find the true religion, we are obligated to tell others and help them to live in touch with reality and the God who is really there. It is a matter of truth, love, and honesty for us to share with others our knowledge of the God who is there, and of what difference this should make in our lives.

Dr. Schaeffer used a common-sense approach to the problem of how we know what is true, and of how we know whether Christianity is true or not. The illustration regarding the silver coin is my own, but he insisted that our beliefs about God must be true to reality. Since Christianity is true to the reality of what really is, we should believe Christianity.

The closer we are to true Christian belief, the closer we are to reality. The farther we are from true Christian belief, the farther we are from reality, or the more inconsistent we are when it comes to what we say we believe and how we act in the world.

Dr. Schaeffer held that if we read the Bible, use our common sense, and look at the world correctly, we should conclude that the teachings of the Bible are true. If, of course, our view of the world is incorrect, we must come to a correct view of the world before we can understand most Christian teaching. Likewise, understanding Christian teaching and living according to the Bible will help us develop a true, common-sense understanding of the world around us, a right way of thinking about all of life, and this right way of thinking reinforces our Christian beliefs and ways of living.

One of the beauties of Dr. Schaeffer's way of teaching about God and Christianity is that he always showed the positive *and* the negative about certain ideas. If he said God was personal, he told what that meant in a positive way and then he also showed what he *didn't* mean by saying *God is personal.* He showed the results of thinking that God is impersonal, as well as personal. He believed that we need to understand both the right and the wrong way of looking at an idea, if we are really going to understand the idea.

Another wonderful thing about his teaching is that he always tried to reduce ideas to their lowest common denominators. For example, he could show that Hinduism, Buddhism, and pantheism have certain things in common at their foundation (that everything is god, and though god is infinite, god is not personal). Then he would show that the Bible teaches that God is both personal and infinite, and that God is also distinct from the world (in the sense that God created the world out of nothing, rather than emanating the world out of himself).[1] He would show how the God of the Bible was different from the god of the pantheist, and how both views could not be right because they were opposite.

He would also show a third alternative: that there is no God, but that the world *just happened to be* (in the sense that there is only time, matter, energy, and chance, but no creator). The fourth alternative, that everything came from nothing (no matter, energy, time, or chance—really *nothing nothing),* he said no one had proposed, because it was really unthinkable.

He insisted that we should look at the three or four different alternatives and compare these with the world, with reality, and with the way we have to live in this world in the practical, everyday affairs of life. We should look at the different religions and how they answer various questions. And then, on the basis of discovering that Christianity is true to the reality of what is, people should accept the Christian faith as true.

Apart from the Bible's teachings, there is no way of really knowing how we in fact know that anything is true. According to most Eastern thinking, all that we see around us is an illusion; this material world is only an illusion, because there is only one reality, and that reality is the Eastern pantheistic god that is impersonal unconsciousness. This means we too are only illusions, no matter what reality tells us about the world and about ourselves. On the basis of Eastern thinking, we have to deny what reality tells us about the world and about ourselves. Reality tells us that we are real and the world is no illusion. If we deny this testimony in favor of Eastern philosophies or Eastern religions, such as Hinduism or Buddhism, in the end we cannot in fact know that anything is true. In short, it is not rational to be a Hindu, Buddhist, or pantheist (a pantheist believes that god is everything and everything is god—Schaeffer calls this "pan-everythingism").

The same problem occurs in the nonbiblical view that the world simply happened to be, and that all that is is here simply because of a combination of time, energy, matter, and chance. In this view *chance* is looked upon as some kind of a *creator;* chance almost becomes some *thing* that creates. But that would imply an act of creation with some sense of direction or purpose or *end in view* for all that is. In this sense, chance becomes personal, because we cannot really conceive of an impersonal beginning. At this point it is more proper to conclude that creation was from a personal beginning, rather than from a chance beginning. To believe that everything was created by chance is not rational. Of course this is an oversimplification, but it does attempt to reduce to absurdity the notion of creation *by chance.*

In reality, a person who believes that everything happens by chance must finally admit that an effect cannot be explained by a cause. In this view, I cannot explain anything I *see* on the basis that there is an object outside of myself making an impact upon my optic nerves. I can't trust anything I *hear,* if everything is simply by chance. Since purpose, direction, and real cause and effect are absent in this view from the very beginning, people who hold this view can't really know anything about what is true or false in reality, or right from wrong. They can't even know that the world was created by chance; they are making a blind leap in the dark. It is an

Dr. Schaeffer at his Rochester, Minnesota, home, discussing his Christian views. Photo courtesy of The Rochester *Post-Bulletin*.

Francis and Edith Schaeffer as young missionaries to Europe in 1950.

Francis and Edith together in their Rochester apartment in January 1979, seven months after he was diagnosed as having cancer.

Dr. and Mrs. Schaeffer with five of their grandchildren: l. to r., Margaret Macaulay, Becky Sandri, Elizabee Sandri, Natasha Middelmann, Kirsty Macaulay. Taken Easter Sunday, 1969.

Francis Schaeffer leading a question-and-answer session at the Auditorium Theatre in Chicago in the spring of 1980.

FROM TOP TO BOTTOM ON THIS SPREAD:

A portion of the long and impressive Reformation Wall and Monument in Geneva, Switzerland. Dr. Schaeffer courageously stood for Reformation principles, naming Farel House for the leader on the left.

A statue of Roger Williams and a quotation from the Mayflower Compact on the Reformation Wall—a reminder to Dr. Schaeffer of the Reformation roots of the United States of America.

A view of the Schaeffer home, Chalet le Chardonnet. The top windows of the chalet are in the office where Dr. Schaeffer worked on many of his books and films.

Chalet les Melezes, the first home of L'Abri in Huemoz, Switzerland. It is now the home of the International Director, Ranald Macaulay, and Susan Schaeffer Macaulay.

Farel House Chapel, Huemoz, Switzerland. The basement houses the study center of tapes and books, while worship is held on the main floor. The Reverend Udo Middelmann is pastor.

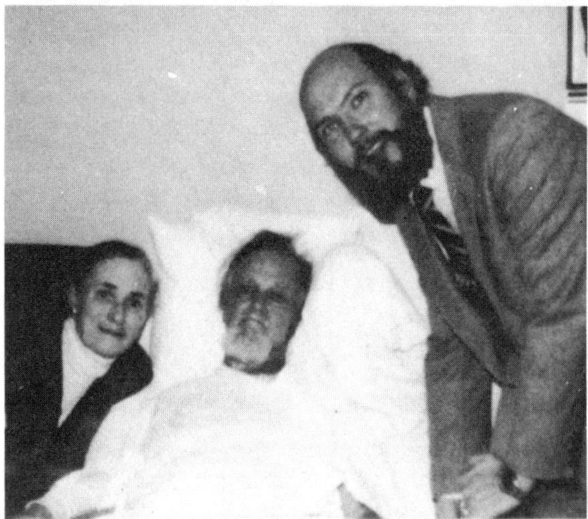

Dr. Schaeffer with the author and four others in a silent, dignified march against abortion. The protest took place in front of the Rochester Methodist Hospital. Photo courtesy of The Rochester *Post-Bulletin,* Merle Dalen, photographer.

The author brought communion to Dr. and Mrs. Schaeffer, Prisca Sandri, and Sue Macaulay at the hospital on New Year's Eve, 1983.

irrational statement of faith to say that everything was created by chance.

Do we really live on the basis of chance? No, we live daily on the basis that things don't happen by chance. We live on the basis that effects *always* have a cause, even though we may not know the cause. From simply turning on a light to starting a car, from eating a sandwich to talking at the lunch counter, we function in a practical, common-sense way on the basis that we live in a real cause-and-effect world.

Does anything happen *by chance* in our world? Only in the sense that *we* do not know its cause. For someone to say all that *is* came from time, energy, and matter, shaped by chance, means simply that he does not know the *cause* of reality. Neither does he know the origin of time, energy, or matter. As we have shown above, if a person is consistent in this belief, he cannot know anything, and in theory he should be unable to turn on a light, start a car, fix a sandwich, or talk to his neighbor. He cannot trust that the light will turn on (barring electrical failure—a *cause* for the switch not to work), that the car will start, that the sandwich will nourish his body, or that his neighbor is really there and can speak sensibly.

The atheist (a person who denies the existence of a god), who tries to explain the world on the basis of *chance,* can't live practically and daily on that basis. The Hindu or the Buddhist has not been able to live consistently believing his fundamental view that ultimate reality, the core of reality, is impersonal unconsciousness. For this reason the Hindu has finite personal gods in the millions, and the Buddhist has different forms of the finite personal Buddha. Only the Bible's teaching about God and reality is consistent with what really is, and the

Christian should live consistently on that basis.

The Christian lives only on the basis that God created the world intentionally, with a reason and a purpose, because he is an intelligent, purposeful, infinite, personal God. And only on the basis of our being created in the image of God, with the ability to reason and comprehend things about the world around us, can we know that anything we know is true or according to reality.

When we look at reality and the three or four basic options that we have for explaining that anything is here, we should be able to convince people that the Bible and the Christian faith are true and right; whereas, opposite beliefs are false and wrong. Of course, in this brief book, I cannot explain in all of their fullness Dr. Schaeffer's arguments for how we know, for how we know that God exists, or for the truth of the Bible and Christianity, but these ideas should help you when you study his books in more detail.[2]

1. See especially his book *Genesis in Space and Time,* in *The Complete Works,* Volume Two, "A Christian View of the Bible As Truth," Book One.

2. See especially Dr. Schaeffer's treatment of these questions in *The God Who Is There, Escape from Reason, He Is There and He Is Not Silent,* and *Back to Freedom and Dignity* in *The Complete Works,* Volume One, "A Christian View Of Philosophy and Culture." For a fuller development of the ideas in the following pages, you must study Dr. Schaeffer's books for yourself. This introduction to his thought follows the outline of his *Basic Bible Studies* (Wheaton: Tyndale House, 1972). I suggest that looking up the Scripture references in that book will give you a more lasting understanding of the Christian system of thought.

8
DOES IT REALLY MATTER?

SUPPOSE you have never traveled to Europe before, and you decide to get your feet wet by going first to Geneva, Switzerland. Upon arriving, you check into your hotel and then go around the corner to one of the many Swiss banks to change your currency into Swiss francs. As you leave the bank, you meet a nicely dressed young man who says that he will give you 100 francs if you will give him 50 francs. Thinking that you can't lose on a deal like that, you give him *all* your francs, and he gives you back double for all you give him.

After he leaves, you look carefully at the strange currency in your hands, and to your surprise, you find that you have a fist full of French francs! Well, you can't spend those in Switzerland, and you hadn't planned to go to France, so back to the bank you go again to get some Swiss francs. You give the cashier 470 French francs, and you receive in return 154 Swiss francs. You are puzzled and concerned, and a little frightened; did someone make a mistake?

You try to explain to the banker that you need 470

Swiss francs, but the teller points out that there is a difference in the exchange rate between Swiss francs and French francs. As a matter of fact, when you leave the bank for the second time, you have just learned a lesson.

When you arrived in Switzerland, suppose you had 100 American dollars. In the bank, you could have exchanged $100 for 235 Swiss francs or 870 French francs! Outside the bank, you changed 235 Swiss francs for 470 French francs, and now you have gone back to the bank, and have in your hands 154 Swiss francs or the equivalent of $65.54. And the nicely dressed young man? He is laughing all the way to another bank!

Of course, in the illustration I have not included the bank charges for all of the exchanges, but I have used representative exchange rates as of this writing. Also, I do not mean to imply that Americans are that dumb or that such a thing could actually happen in Switzerland! But let me ask you, *does it really matter* whether you have 470 Swiss francs or 470 French francs, wherever you are?

Apart from the use of different currencies and other such *practical* concerns, we tend to think that *ideas* don't really matter. Some of us have been taught that all religions are basically the same and that faith is just a matter of personal opinion. Some people think that your faith should be whatever meets your individual needs. We have been brainwashed, by repetitive pronouncements, to believe that all religions are but different paths to the same God, that different religions are just different boxcars on the same train going the same place. If we believe this, however, we do so either because we have not studied the different religions deeply, or because we have never seen or experienced the destructive effects of different religious views and forms of faith. Maybe we have even convinced ourselves that a loving and intelligent God doesn't really care what anybody believes about him or about reality!

Different religions have in common the use of the word *god,* but they mean very different things by the use of that word. Bible-believing Christians and liberals have in common the use of the word *God,* but they mean radically different things by the use of that name. These uses make a practical difference, and if you don't know the difference, you can be short changed, and not even know it!

You cannot function well in Europe if you do not know the difference between the various currencies and if you cannot figure out the exchange rates and methods for purchasing things in the different countries. Unless you are totally isolated from the rest of the world, you cannot function well in the world unless you know the *practical* difference belief in different religions can make.

I am not speaking simply of faith in the true God as the only path to heaven (a claim most religions have in common, even as they disagree about who the true god really is); rather, Christianity and the other religions are either true to the world as it is or they are not. The truth or the falsehood of the ideas we hold about God make a practical difference in the way we treat others, ourselves, and the world in which we live, as well as an eternal difference.

Two different views about man and the world are engraved on two different coins. The French 10-franc coin has engraved in French, "Liberty, Equality, and Fraternity," the slogan of the French Revolution and a basic idea of the Enlightenment. In France, the ideas of the

Enlightenment were practiced; Reason was elevated as the savior of man and placed above the God of the Bible. Reason was deified, called "god." The French Revolution began shortly after the American Revolution. The French Revolution took on a decidedly anti-Christian and antichurch flavor, and it ended with an internal bloodbath and the dictatorship of Napoleon.[1] The slogan on the French franc represents ideas that have changed the world, as man with his reason thought he could do things very well in opposition to God or without God; this is the basic premise of what we call "humanism" today. We need to realize that the only real path to "Liberty, Equality, and Fraternity" (a worthy ideal) is through the honest practice of biblical principles in society.

The other coin is the Swiss 5-franc coin. On it is engraved in Latin, "The Lord Shall Provide." With these two coins we find a radical difference between ideas that are God-centered, which see the proper relationship of the Lord to man, and the ideas of the Enlightenment, which are man-centered. Notice, the coin doesn't use the Latin word for "god"; rather, it is specific. "The Lord" refers to the God of the Bible, specifically to the Lord Jesus Christ. Switzerland was founded on Reformation ideas, the ideas of Luther, Calvin, Bèze, Knox, and Farel, as they tried to apply the Bible's teaching to society. Farel rode on horseback through the Alps and through the tiny village of Huémoz, promoting the Reformation four hundred years before Dr. Schaeffer arrived there to base a work called L'Abri on Reformation ideas.

Switzerland has one of the strongest democracies in the world, and it includes four distinct groups of people with four distinct languages being used within its borders. The people cooperate in their government, but you can tell the different parts of Switzerland immediately; it is as easy as reading the *official* writing on the bathroom doors!

The real difference between France and Switzerland, even today, can be traced to the different *foundations* of each country. The Reformation wasn't perfect, but building a society or a life upon the God of the Bible makes a radical difference from building a society or a life upon man alone with his finite reason.

Christians should be radicals in the sense that we look at the *roots* of different philosophical ideas and religious beliefs and then insist that people build their lives upon the foundation the God of the Bible provides. There is no contradiction between faith and sound reason. Christians should reason with people, and show them how sensible it is to follow the God of the Bible and his principles.

Dr. Schaeffer knew the importance and the difference, from firsthand observation, between building a society on biblical principles or upon humanistic principles. He demonstrated in *How Should We Then Live?* and *The Christian Manifesto* that America, like Switzerland, was founded on a biblical consensus, and specifically upon Reformation ideas.

We can see the difference this makes today when we compare Christianity with the ideas of *humanism,* the philosophy that believes only in man and what his reason can know and achieve for the world. It denies the existence of God and tries to destroy the influence of any god-centered religion upon society.

True Christianity seeks pluralism within society, a pluralism that allows for the free discussion of ideas in a true democracy, where there is tremendous freedom, but within the moral boundaries set by God in the Bible. Christians believe that in the marketplace of ideas they can demonstrate the superiority of Christian ideas; therefore, Christians are not afraid to discuss their beliefs with others and promote freedom of speech. Christianity teaches that God has given us moral boundaries for the public good or for the good of society, as well as for the good of each individual. Christians stand up for biblical absolutes in the essential areas of public morality, because we know that in doing so we are preserving good government, our society, and our culture.

On the other hand, humanism, the foundation for both liberalism and communism, seeks to deny religious ideas a voice in the marketplace of ideas, especially in the public schools. Humanism opposes people who, for religious reasons, want to legislate morality *for the public good.* Humanism wages battle using the slogan "You can't legislate morality" to convince people (who don't realize that all legislation is the legislation of some person's or some group's morality or immorality) to promote a permissiveness that will eventually destroy the public good and every democracy *from within.* As a society breaks up from the excesses of permissivism, excesses that do not respect the rights of others, it often calls for a totalitarian leader to make things right. Totalitarianism usually flows from humanism. We need look only at history and at the many communist and facist governments to illustrate that conclusion. Dr. Schaeffer argues the point persuasively in *How Should We Then Live?, Whatever Happened to the Human Race?* and *The Christian Manifesto.*[2]

Since humanism is based upon man and only man's ideas, it has no basis for absolute truth and falsehood, right and wrong. A consistent humanist should be lost in a sea of relativity, and he has lost much of his ability to reason. Denying the existence of God, he has no real explanation for why the world and man are here, or why anything is right or wrong; therefore, everything is permitted, or should be. He must base his morality and the laws he tries to make on simple majority opinion, or worse, on what some elite ruling class thinks is best for society. Whenever a country has had a totally humanistic base, great inhumanities and atrocities have always followed. Because the leaders and the people no longer have the ability to distinguish good from bad, they abuse one another.

We saw in the previous chapter that there is absolute truth and absolute right and wrong, based upon the way man reasons as created in the image of God, based upon the reality of the world as it really is as created by God. When the humanist denies the existence of God, he soon loses his ability to reason soundly. The closer people move toward the God of the Bible, the less they are persuaded by the arguments of the humanist. The closer people move toward the use of sound and practical reason, the closer they can move toward the God of the Bible and reality, and the easier it is to see humanism and its results for what they really are.

When we look around us, we can see the results of practicing humanistic ideas and turning from Christianity. We can see what happens to a culture and a society that excludes Christian ideas from public policy and is no longer Christian. Every type of destructive debauchery is practiced and permitted. The society and the culture begin to crumble. No one seems to know how to turn things around, as they become disgusted with child molestation and other perversions. Gone is the moral form that allowed freedom without the license that abuses self and others. Everything has been tried, except returning to God and the Christian faith and practice, and mankind is too proud to admit that it can't make it without God and his help. Does it really matter what we profess and what we practice?

1. This is something you can read more about in *How Should We Then Live?* in *The Complete Works,* Volume Five, "A Christian View of the West," Book Two.

2. Ibid.

9
LIBERALISM OR CHRISTIANITY?

SEVERAL YEARS AGO a good and wise man built a large brick house upon a high mountain. He anchored its foundation in the solid granite, and then he opened his doors to all in need. He even went out to find the needy, that he might bring them into his home for help. Many people came to his doors, and many found help for their problems. The man was so good and wise that no matter what the problem, if people followed his advice, their problem was solved! He led them to believe in God, and he showed them that following the God of the Bible would make a lasting difference in their lives here and hereafter, no matter where they were. People were happy and joyful in their relationship with God, with the man, and with one another. They went out and began to change the world! Some of them even went to build other homes on a good foundation, with sound teachings, just like his.

Then the man died. Those who inherited his home were not as good or as wise. They decided to move the big house down to the beach at the foot of the mountain and to convince others to move their homes too. After all, they thought, it will be easier to move this house than to build a new one. And since people around the world know to come to this house to solve their problems, we will be able to keep the house open with all the money they will bring. Since the beach is a lovely, warm place to relax, and the mountain is so hard to climb, more people will surely come to help us pay the bills! Since the Bible is *so* hard to understand and teach, we will just teach our own ideas or tell people that any god will solve their problems *if they just have enough faith and think positive!* If we need to, we'll just *make up* what the Bible means. Since it is hard and expensive to dig a good foundation, we will just set this good and sturdy house down in the sand, and everything will be all right.

But they had a problem. What about all those nice people already in the house? Would they want to move to the beach? No, probably not, because they loved the view and the brisk mountain air that helped them keep their minds clear and focused upon the truth. And so the new owners of the home convinced everyone in the house that they needed to repaint all of the walls, temporarily board up the windows (especially while painting), and replace all the woodwork and the ceilings. With all the work being done to fix things up, so much noise was made by the workers inside the house that they didn't even know when the movers came to move the house to the beach. To this very day, many of these same people are still working and happily celebrating their very successful restoration projects, but they don't even know that their nice brick house has been moved! There hasn't even been a really serious storm at the beach—yet!

This parable describes the liberal takeover of the mainline churches at the turn of the twentieth century. With denominational leaders, seminary administrators, and professors in most mainline churches solidly liberal, they carry on their programs of subverting biblical Christianity *from within.* They train the new flock of liberal pastors to follow them as their shepherds, rather than to follow *the* Shepherd. They insist that their constituents pay the bills, based upon their memory of all the good that used to be done. They often use the words *God* and *Jesus* and *Savior,* not because they mean what the Bible means by those words, but to continue to evoke the fond memories of their followers (especially whenever they think they might be getting wise to their charade). Whenever anyone seems to be getting wise and starts to raise a critical question, they are reminded by their shepherds, "Judge not, lest ye be judged!" Dr. Schaeffer said, "Liberalism is nothing more than humanism dressed up in religious terminology."

This parable also describes the process now going on within many of the evangelical churches in the 1980s. Dr. Schaeffer lived through the liberal takeover of the mainline churches, and he saw how the battle to preserve the Christian faith was poorly fought. He deplored all the lack of love in the battle, but he continued to fight in the battle, a battle for truth. A few years before his death, he saw the liberal takeover begin again, but this time within the evangelical churches. This new takeover distressed him greatly; therefore, he said of his book *The Great Evangelical Disaster,* "The statement I am making in the pages of this book is perhaps the most important statement I have ever made."[1]

The next eleven brief chapters in this book will describe the teachings of biblical Christianity, but you must understand that these teachings are opposite from the teachings of liberalism, the new liberalism as well as the old liberalism. One set of teachings must be right and the other set of teachings must be wrong. Put another way, one set of teachings is biblical Christianity, and the other set is destructive error. One is in touch with reality, and the other is unrealistic. These teachings make an eternal difference, as well as an historical difference. Ideas do matter!

Followers of liberalism, neo-orthodoxy, liberation theology, and process theology have one thing in common. They do not believe the Bible is true in all that it affirms! They do not believe God has spoken without error in the Bible! They try to prove it, and then they try to live as though it doesn't make any real difference!

The foundation for the Church is the teachings of the apostles and the prophets, with Jesus Christ as the chief Cornerstone; in other words, the Bible. When the foundation is destroyed or discredited by any of the methods used in the theologies mentioned above, then true Christian faith and the verifiability of the Christian faith are also destroyed. The practice of Christianity is also weakened or destroyed.

It is absolutely essential for us to look at the foundation of different belief systems. It is especially important for us to make certain that our church is staying on the foundation provided by the God of the Bible. The psalmist asks us, "When the foundations are being destroyed, what can the righteous do?" (Psalm 11:3). We must not become as those in the house, who tinkered with the plans, programs, and policies given them by their leaders so they wouldn't know what was really going on. All the time they were blindly maintaining their leaders' destructive work, and they didn't even know it! The liberals make every attempt to sound "Christian" to the people in the pews, to keep them busy, to keep them thinking about "evangelism," to keep the money rolling in, so they in turn can build a church and a society upon a humanistic foundation, miles away from the foundation provided by the God who is there.

Let's try to keep it simple. Sometimes the liberals teach that in spite of all the errors, God's living Word still gets through somehow and makes a personal encounter with the reader. But how can I know the personal encounter is *really* from God if I have no objective standard to measure it by? Only a revelation from God that is without error can give me a standard to know if my ideas and "feelings" are really from him. The Bible is that standard—God's revelation without error. Sometimes the liberals teach that you just need to read the Bible until you have an "aha" reaction, and then you have the Word of God. But what has a person read for an hour, if in the process he has had no "aha" reaction? Sometimes they will say that the Bible "contains" the Word of God, *but the Bible is not "the Word of God."* Then they will use a lot of intellectual gymnastics to try to prove that what they've found in the Bible is really "the Word of God," and not just their subjective opinion. Their approach is man-centered, humanistic; hence, Schaeffer always returned to the point that liberalism was simply humanism dressed in sheeps' clothing.

Usually, the liberals teach that the Bible is simply man's written aspirations about God and the universe that he has compiled over the years. In other words, they teach that the Bible has a humanistic base, that man just began with his reason and experience to describe God over the years, and that the Bible is just another attempt at a human description of an unknowable divine reality. They argue, "You can't understand God!" They deny that God has spoken real words and sentences and that these real words and sentences give us real truth about who he is as well as real truth about reality and history (what is called propositional truth or propositional revelation). They deny that God spoke and acted in history in such a way that man could verify his words and actions and then know that the words and actions were really from the God who is there. At the other extreme, some have even taught that the writings of Paul Tillich and other liberals should be added to the Bible. "After all," they argue from the other side of their mouths, "has God stopped speaking to us?"

The authority of the Bible and the means of interpreting the Bible were the crucial problems that faced the mainline churches at the turn of the century, and the mainline churches were subsequently destroyed by liberal subversion. These are the fundamental issues that face the evangelical churches today. Dr. Schaeffer wondered why the evangelical churches didn't learn from the errors of the past. Once the Bible's inerrancy was dismissed, the liberals in the mainline churches began to question publicly (and with very little real resistance within the church) the Bible's teaching on the virgin birth of Christ, the miracles of Jesus, the teachings of Jesus on certain *private* moral questions, the historical resurrection of Jesus, his death on behalf of sinful mankind, and his second coming, among other doctrines. Almost everything that the cults deny about God and Jesus, the mainline churches have been denying for years! The people in the mainline pews don't even know why they are dying both spiritually and numerically. The liberal mainline churches today are far more destructive than any cults, because they have credibility the cults don't have, while they teach the same soul-destroying doctrines.

In his books Dr. Schaeffer deals with all these issues thoroughly. He approaches biblical Christianity, and how we should interpret the Bible, from the philosophical, the theological, and the historical perspective (or from what is called "biblical evidences"). He wrote the books *Genesis in Space and Time* and *Joshua in the Flow of Biblical History* to show the importance of knowing that the Bible is both historical and inerrant in all it affirms, and that this belief can be verified. Regarding the historicity of the whole Bible from the discoveries in archaeology, for example, he included excellent material on the subject in *Whatever Happened to the Human Race?*[2]

The liberals have been asked, "If the Bible can't be trusted in the areas of science and history, how can you trust it in the religious and moral areas?" Some have honestly answered, "We can't, and we don't!" This is one reason the liberals see so very little difference between Christianity and the pagan religions, and why so little evangelism is performed by their missionaries. Most missionary work by the liberal churches is little more than social and political activism.

We need to ask ourselves these questions: If the foundation for the church has been destroyed in some churches, to the extent that some can't even really know objectively any truths about the Christian faith, what do we have left? Of what value is it to tinker with the church's insides, when the foundation has been destroyed and disaster, though postponed, will inevitably follow? How many "good works" can a church built on sand perform to make up for its loss of faith in the

Jesus Christ of the Bible? How many people are going to be destroyed by liberalism before the building tumbles down and destroys those left inside? When are those still inside going to wake up? What will they do if they do wake up? Will the "evangelical churches" have anything left to offer them, if they do wake up?

Isn't it time that we learn clearly what the Bible teaches about God and what a full salvation in Jesus Christ means, so that we might be able to save some, and so that we might not be misled as we fight the battle for truth in our time?

1. Since this book was released in March of 1984, advertisements for the book have appeared in most leading evangelical magazines. These advertisements include this quotation. *The Great Evangelical Disaster* (Westchester: Crossway Books, 1984).

2. *The Complete Works,* Volume Five.

10
THE GOD OF THE BIBLE

WHERE DO WE BEGIN a systematic study of Christian truth? Where the Bible begins: "In the beginning God" (Genesis 1:1). The Bible tells us there is one God. This is the consistent teaching of both the Old and New Testaments. There is one God, but God is three Persons. We are not to think of God as the mathematical formula: one equals three. Rather, God is one in essence: God is Spirit; God is Light; God is Love. But in another sense, God is three Persons.

In Genesis 1 we read, "God created," "the Spirit of God was hovering," and "God said, 'Let us make man in our image.' " In John 1 we read, "In the beginning was the Word, and the Word was with God, and the Word was God . . . Through him all things were made." From the beginning of Christianity, Christians claimed that they were worshiping the God of the Old Testament, and that in the Old Testament they found evidence that allowed them to be consistent with the Old Testament when they taught that God was three Persons. They also believed that they were being true to the teachings of Jesus, their Lord and Savior.

When Jesus told his disciples to go into all the world, he told them to teach and baptize "in the name [singular] of the Father and of the Son and of the Holy Spirit" (Matthew 28:19). At the Great Commission, Jesus told his disciples once again that there is one God, but this one God who is there is in reality three Persons: Father, Son, and Holy Spirit. His disciples were commanded to go out and teach *all* that he commanded, and this certainly included teaching who God is in three Persons.

When Jesus prayed to God, calling him "Abba," he was calling God by his real name, "Father." It isn't that Jesus used *the name* "Abba" (Daddy) when he prayed, as though this were just another name for God among many. Rather, when Jesus prayed "Abba," he did so because God is really "Father," and in a special sense God is really "Jesus' Father" *in reality.* When Jesus prayed to God as his Father, he was also telling us something he wanted us to know about the real nature and character of God. "God is Father, and God is Jesus' Father," is a true proposition about the God who is really there. When Jesus told his disciples that they could pray, "Our Father," he was telling them something about the nature and the character of God that could make a real difference in the way they prayed and lived in relation to God.

When Jesus told his disciples he would send them another Comforter, he was speaking about the Holy Spirit. The Holy Spirit is the Person of God who is sent to indwell the believing Christian. The Holy Spirit is not an "it" or a "she," but as the Spirit of Christ and of the Father, the Holy Spirit is "he." The Holy Spirit is personal. He speaks, and we can grieve him by our words and actions. The Holy Spirit gives us a relationship with God and a power we couldn't have before Jesus was crucified, dead, buried, and raised from the dead.

Before Jesus' crucifixion, the Apostle John reports this incident between Jesus and the Jews who did not believe in him:

> "I tell you the truth," Jesus answered, "before Abraham was born, I am!" At this they picked up stones to stone him, but Jesus hid himself, slipping away from the temple grounds. (John 8:58, 59)

The Jews picked up the stones as a punishment for blasphemy, because they knew Jesus was telling them "*I am* God." "I am" is the holy name of God, which God gave to Moses when Moses asked him about who he should say had sent him to the Jews in Egypt. Jesus' use of "I am" is a special feature of John's Gospel, and Jesus uses "I am" several times to make this point about his identity with God.

Jesus claimed to be God, and either he was or he wasn't. If he was, we know something wonderful about God and his great love for us. If he wasn't, Jesus was either deranged or an evil blasphemer. But people who deny he is God almost universally admit that Jesus was one of the world's greatest ethical teachers. Deranged blasphemers are not accorded that honor, and so the idea that he was deranged or a blasphemer simply is not rational. Jesus' claims about himself and Christianity's claims about Jesus are either true or false. Jesus' claims are true to reality or they are not. They are either true to the Old Testament or they are not. Christians claim that they and Jesus are true to the teachings of both the Old and New Testaments, as well as true to reality.

Christianity says that Jesus is God and the Holy Spirit is God and the Father is God, but Christianity refuses to believe in more than one God. Christianity teaches that in one sense there is one God, but in another sense God is three Persons.

When Jesus was baptized by John, we see God in three Persons in one place. Jesus was baptized in the water, his Father declared from heaven, "This is my Son, whom I love; with him I am well pleased," and the Spirit of God descended like a dove and lighted on Jesus (Matthew 3:16, 17).

Christianity stands or falls in the truth of the reality that there is one God in three Persons. In his essence, God is personal and in a personal relationship with himself, as each Person of the Trinity loves and communicates with each other Person.

But what about the person who doesn't believe in the Bible? Or what about the liberal, who teaches that Jesus didn't really claim to be God, that the New Testament writers just put these words in Jesus' mouth to make him look great, and then tried to justify their claims about him? What about the cults that honor Jesus and teach about him, but, like the liberal, deny his deity?

Francis Schaeffer could still talk to these people. He first approached the person where he was, and asked him to explain his beliefs. He showed love and respect for the other person's personality, as created in the image of God no matter what he said he was. And he prayed that what he said about the God who is there might make a difference in the other person's beliefs.

If the problem was not understanding the Bible's teaching, he taught what the Bible taught, as I have briefly outlined it above. If the problem was one of comparative religions, as he talked to a Hindu for example, he showed how the Christians' God compared to the Hindus' gods as well as to their pantheistic god. If the problem was a cult teaching, he would approach the person according to the cult's teaching. On the other hand, if the problem was of a philosophical nature, he could show how belief in the Trinity answered the philosophical questions. All these methods are used in his books and tapes.

To answer some of the standard questions about the Trinity, Dr. Schaeffer would say that belief in the Trinity means that God has always existed in a personal, loving relationship as three Persons. God is whole and complete. God did not *need to create* in order to have something to love or relate to. God created from his own free will and not from necessity. Personality and personal relationship are at the core or root of existence in God himself; therefore, we live in a personal rather than an impersonal universe. Created in the image of God, man has a reason for the personality he feels and cannot deny; man has a reason for his need to be in a relationship with some other person. Created in the image of God, man has a reason for his own creativity. The Trinity answers the questions modern man poses. Christians didn't invent the Trinity to answer modern man's questions, but Christians discovered that the doctrine of the Trinity (which they found in the Bible) answers modern man's questions and solves his problems.

The existence of the Trinity makes it reasonable for us to believe that God can have a relationship with us that includes speaking to us and telling us true things about himself and the world. As a matter of fact, this is what we should expect from God—a personal communication from him to us and from us to him. Just as we can't know everything about another person, we shouldn't expect to know God exhaustively. But just as we can know some true things about another person by his words and actions, so we should expect to know some true things from a personal God who can speak and act.

The existence of the Trinity also answers the philosophical question of the one and the many. Is reality at its root or foundation *one* (monism) or *many* (pluralism)? If reality is one, how do we have the existence of or explain the existence of particulars (individual objects are "particulars")? If "what really is" is one, are particular things—such as you, I, and the sky—just an illusion (the answer Hinduism gives, for example)? If reality at its foundation is many, what gives each particular its meaning? Where did the many come from? How did the many things get here? Philosophers, trusting in their reason alone and beginning only from themselves, without a revelation from God, have not been able to give adequate answers to the problem of the existence of the one and the many, of monism and pluralism. We find the answer in the Bible.

The doctrine of the Trinity answers the problem by saying that at the root of existence is God, and the nature of God is both one and many. There is one God, but this one God has always existed as three Persons, and this one God created a world outside of himself, in the sense that the world is not an extension of God. The particulars, the many, have their real existence and their meaning explained on the basis of having been created intentionally by a personal God, who created them for a purpose which he has shared in part with the personal man whom he also created.

Without an inerrant Bible, Christians cannot answer the questions modern man asks, questions that reality poses for him, questions that should drive him to the conclusion that God exists, but then to ask, "What kind of a God is the God who is there?" For this reason, among others, Dr. Schaeffer fought for the inerrancy of Scripture. Likewise, the fact that the Bible answers so well the modern questions people have is a good argument for its inspiration and authority.

It is reasonable to expect that God is able and willing to tell true things to us about himself and reality, and to do so in a way that protects the individual personality of the Bible writers, while protecting the accuracy of his Word written! *It is reasonable for us to expect* that he would do nothing less!

11
BEGINNING AT THE BEGINNING

"IN THE BEGINNING God created the heavens and the earth. . . . Then God said, 'Let us make man in our image, in our likeness, and let them rule over the fish of the sea and the birds of the air, over the livestock, over all the earth, and over all the creatures that move along the ground.' So God created man in his own image, in the image of God he created him; male and female he created them" (Genesis 1:1, 26, 27).

Dr. Schaeffer insisted on numerous occasions that if we are telling people about Christianity, we don't begin with Jesus and his death upon the cross; we must begin at the beginning with Genesis. We must tell them about the God who is there and show them that he is not the liberal's god or the god of Eastern thinking. Next, we must show them that God created the world, not as an extension of himself, but as a real objective universe. And then we must show them that God made man in his image, and this means God made a significant man in a significant history. Man is not a zero. Man is not determined. Man is responsible, and he can make choices that will cause ripples throughout eternity. And then we must show them that man has fallen and they have sinned; therefore, they need a Savior.

We have seen that it is not reasonable to believe that *chance* created the world. Chance does not explain the existence of what is. Chance does not explain why matter and energy exist and why there is duration of matter and energy we call time.

The world must have been created by God. But what kind of God created the world, and what kind of a world is this?

Eastern or pantheistic thinking says the world is an extension of their god's being and essence; you are god and I am god, along with the fishes, the birds, and the rocks. In some process theology this also means that god is growing and improving just as we are; everything is getting better and better. In some of the Eastern religions, all of the particulars that exist are simply illusions, because their god is the one and the one is god. You and I are just illusions, but *whose* illusions, ours or god's? One Eastern guru is reported to have suggested that murder is okay, because in a murder you are only destroying an illusion. In that sense, murder even becomes a great benefit to everyone involved!

The presence of evil in the world is a problem for the pantheist. Does the existence of evil mean that his god is both good and evil? On what basis can we have morals and encourage right behavior if all that exists is simply illusion, and if *the only one reality* (the unconscious, impersonal Eastern god) doesn't even know that we exist or that we know the difference between reality and illusion or between good and evil? In fact, in consistent Eastern thinking, we don't exist, because we are only illusions. We were never objectively created and given any opportunity to do anything significant. We can throw stones, but the ripples aren't real! There is no real answer in Eastern or pantheistic thinking for why things are as they are, or for what we know to be true as we observe reality. It is not reasonable to be a pantheist, and Eastern religions deplore the use of reason. Only historic biblical Christianity respects man and his ability to reason.

The only other alternative god worth discussing in this book is the alternative offered by the deists. In the Age of Reason, the Enlightenment, the deists taught that God had created the universe like a clock that kept perfect time because it was designed by a superior clockmaker. Beginning with the view that everything should be understood mathematically, the deists were forced to conclude that God had created and regulated the world so that it would proceed mechanically without his involvement. They ruled out miracles and other special acts of God, including the giving of a revelation to man (the Bible as God's Word written). Future events, then, were predictable on the basis of earlier events.

According to the deists, God is not a prayer-answering God and he is not involved in our lives in any way. The universe runs along very well without him. But in this view, man is just a mechanical piece in the clock, a part of the cosmic machine. Man is determined to fulfill his function as created by the great clockmaker, because he is stuck inside the clock as a part of the clock, and God is stuck outside the clock. Man has no free will, no responsibility, and is not accountable for his actions. Man just ticks on and on. The universe as a clock means that we are only mechanical men. Here man is a zero. Man is not significant in a significant history. Deism is not a reasonable explanation for the universe or the existence of man.

With this as background, to *begin at the beginning* means that according to the Bible, God created the objective world. He created man to inhabit that world, so man could use the endowments he had been given as created in the image of God. God created an objective, finite world, or *cosmos*. This means the world had a beginning in time and it will have an ending in time; the world also depends upon God for its continuing existence. God is infinite, and he depends upon no power outside of his own power. God has no beginning and he will never end. In the sense of God being infinite and the cosmos being finite, there is a great chasm between God and creation. On the other hand, there is a great chasm between personality and impersonality, that is, between God and being created in the image of God, and the rest of creation. God is dissimilar from man and the world in the area of God being infinite and man being finite. But God and man are dissimilar from the world in the sense that God and man are both personal and the world is not personal.

How do we know all these things? We know because the infinite/personal God, who is really there, has told finite/personal man, who objectively exists as created by God. The personal/infinite God has spoken, and man has recorded God's Word in the Bible. What we know about God from the Bible, what we know about God's nature and his character, is consistent with what we know about the world as it is, and with what we know about our own nature and aspirations. We know why the world is here and why it is the way it is, because God has spoken to man; one personality has spoken to another personality. If God is as the Bible describes him to be, this is what we should expect from God and it should not seem unusual to us.

The infinite/personal God has spoken to finite/personal man. God has spoken truly, but he has not spoken exhaustively. There is room for real science to take place. There is room for us to investigate the universe to learn more about it, and there is a reason to investigate the universe. We know that the universe is objectively there; it is not an illusion, but real. God has not spoken exhaustively, but we can know true things about the nature and character of God because he has spoken. We are finite and he is infinite; therefore, even throughout eternity as we learn more about the God who is there, we will not exhaust him or ever know all about him. We will know many true things about God and the universe, but we will never know everything; in this sense, God and the universe will always be mysterious to us, but not unknown or unknowable.

God created the objective universe, and he placed man in it, an unprogrammed man and an unprogrammed woman. He placed the earth and everything in and of the earth under their rule or lordship. He gave them one rule to obey, but they rebelled against God and broke the one rule. For this reason, we live in a fallen world.

Our world is not the same as God created it. God created the world good, and he evaluated the world and called every aspect of his creation "good." But man rebelled against God, and evil entered the world. Adjustments were made in the world by God to punish man and to inhibit both his continued sinning and his evil imaginings through too much leisure time.

Man and woman made history, real history, history

that would affect their every descendant. They could have made good history, but they chose to make bad history. The history they made would necessitate God's taking drastic actions in the future to make things right again.

Created in the image of God, they were creative people, but they began using their creativity with a rebellious spirit or attitude. God didn't punish them for breaking some trite little rule. God punished them because they began to use their creativity in rebellion, rather than in the many good and right ways he had described to them after creating them. He had warned them, "If you disobey me, then you will know both good and evil by personal experience." By giving unprogrammed man the opportunity to obey him or disobey him, God was respecting man's nature as he had created him. When man freely chose to disobey God, he failed to respect his Creator and Sustainer. As supreme Governor of the universe, God has to punish rebellious children.

Historic biblical Christianity has an explanation for the fact of evil in the world. Evil wasn't caused by God; evil was caused by a significant man who was tempted by a significant woman who was tempted by a significant tempter (Satan). The first chapters of Genesis show that man's choices are real; they make a difference. Man is significant.

Adam and Eve willfully chose to disobey God, and they had to accept the consequences. Their decision has affected all of us, just as our decisions affect people we don't even know down through history. Adam and Eve committed the original sin, and we have had to live with the evil consequences ever since. And each of us has sinned. We have to live with the evil consequences of our own actions, and our evil actions cause harm to others too. Satan has declared an all-out war on God and his creation, including God's people, and we have to suffer the consequences.

Historic biblical Christianity has an explanation for death. God promised Adam and Eve that they would die if they rebelled against him. Prior to Adam and Eve's sin there was no death anywhere on earth. Their rebellion affected the life of every living creature. Adam and Eve learned by experience the horrible significance of rebellion in a significant universe. By personal experience they learned how horrible evil is in contrast to how good God had made their world. We know it too, from hindsight. When Adam and Eve sinned, death entered the world. Death is a horrible evil; death is a part of the abnormal world we live in, not as created by God, but as a part of God's justice in a fallen world. Death entered the whole world when Adam and Eve rebelled, because God needed to warn us of the horrible consequences we and the whole world suffer every time we rebel and disobey him.

But death is not God's final word to fallen man.

12
WHAT'S THE PROBLEM?

"WHAT AM I? Am I an animal or a machine or simply *nothing?* Do I really matter? Am I important? Does anybody really care about me? Why do I feel as if I am being crushed between the wheels of the cosmos, with nobody at the controls? Do I live in a silent universe, where these questions cannot be answered?"

The Bible declares: "You [God] made him [mankind] a little lower than the heavenly beings [or *than God]* and crowned him with glory and honor. You made him ruler over the works of your hands; you put everything under his feet " (Psalm 8:5, 6). What a difference the Word of God makes! God made us in his image, and for a purpose. There is meaning for life at the very foundation of all things. God has not been silent! We can know who we are, who is at the controls, and where it's all going!

Dr. Schaeffer repeated over and over again, "Man is who he is, no matter what he says he is. He is created in the image of the infinite/personal God who is there." We are finite, personal miniatures of the God who created all that is. If we say we are only animals or machines or *nothing,* and if we try to live on that basis, we cannot do so consistently in the world God has made for us to live in.

One of God's great and wonderful graces is his shutting us up to living in the reality he has created. Reality confronts us with who we really are and who God really is, no matter what we say we are. If we try to live according to false ideas about God and the world, reality will challenge us. Butting our heads up against the world as God created it should make us think. When we think we are only animals or machines or simply nothing, we are out of touch with reality, with the real world as it is.

God created mankind both male and female. He created each person both body and soul. Each person is both material and spiritual. Our bodies are carefully crafted machines that God created good. But we are so much more than well-oiled machines with a soul. We have many things in common with the animals, but we are more than higher primates.

Some have taught that our bodies are evil, matter is evil, and this material world is evil. They have the notion that our souls are *trapped* in machine-like bodies, and that this is our fate until death frees us. Scientific and philosophical inquiry has led mankind to many valid discoveries about the physical world and man, but we are more than the eye can see or the mind can imagine.

The Book of Genesis reports that God created the world, and then evaluated his workmanship. "God saw all that he had made, and it was very good" (Genesis 1:31). Our problem is not *how we were made.* Our problem is that something happened after we were made! The Bible says mankind chose to rebel against

God, and most are still rebelling. We have a moral problem. We have rebelled against God. We are suffering because our rebellion has brought death.

The word *death* means "separation." When Adam and Eve sinned, they died spiritually. They were separated from God spiritually; they lost their close personal relationship with him. And God told them that at some point in the future they would die physically; the soul would depart from the body, and the body would return to the dust from which God had created it. God had warned them beforehand that death would be the result of rebellion, and he had to bring forth the consequences they deserved.

If God had not acted consistently with his Word regarding the first human pair, other intelligent beings, the angels, for example, and those born after Adam and Eve, could have concluded that God is a liar and does not keep his word, or that they could rebel too and not suffer the consequences. Rebels always mistake compassion for leniency! Later, other rebels could have raised their angry fists and screamed, "But you didn't punish Adam and Eve! You aren't fair! You can't punish me!"

In addition to spiritual and physical death, there is a third death as well. If individual men and women continue in their rebellion against God, then they will spend eternity separated from his presence. Only God can provide the solution for all three deaths that mankind may suffer.

When we say that man is fallen and that we live in a fallen world, we mean that the world and man are now imperfect. The world is not now as God created it. Down to our very genes and chromosomes, we are fallen, imperfect. But we do not mean that fallen man is now dead, insignificant and incapable of making real choices that affect a real history. We are fallen, but we are not zeros. We are still important and valuable; we are responsible for our actions.

At some point, every person revolts against God and dies spiritually. Unless Christ comes before we die physically, all of us will experience the departing or the separating of our souls from our bodies. We are so valuable, as created in the image of God, that our souls will never die. Unless we are reconciled to God, we will live for eternity completely apart from him.

The Christian answer explains what modern man sees all around him. The Bible explains why death pervades all of life. Modern man cannot discover the answers to his deepest questions and longings apart from the Bible's teaching.

Since the fallen state of our world is so apparent to everyone, we should ask ourselves: "What are my capabilities? Can I solve these problems?"

The Bible says that having been created good and in the image of God, I am now a fallen, imperfect person living in an imperfect world. But what about my abilities, if everything is fallen now! Do I have the ability to learn about God and have a relationship with him? Can I find a meaning for life? We are fallen, but the image of God that we bear has not been totally erased. We can still reason, express emotions, create, and love—but not perfectly.

Dr. Schaeffer said there are three possible answers to the questions about whether or not fallen man can find God and meaning for life, and about *how* he can find God and subsequently meaning for life.

First (in my own phrasing), we could say this: There is really no significant problem! I can begin with my reason alone, and on the basis of *reason alone,* I can understand everything I need to know. On the basis of simply looking around, by examining myself and the world in which I live (on the basis of what is called *natural revelation),* I can reason myself to God and understand him, if I want to. I can find meaning for living with or without God. I don't need any special help or special revelation from God to find him or discover a purpose for living.

This is the attitude of a man who wants to be autonomous and independent; it is the attitude Adam and Eve chose over against God. This is the attitude of most modern men and women. But on the basis of their reason alone, many have come to admit that they have not been able to find God or any reason for living. Therefore, they have abandoned reason, and they now seek God or meaning in the irrational (which means, they seek God or meaning for life on the level of feelings or experiences that cannot be explained). Many people, then, begin to advocate answers to life that are completely irrational and based only on experiences or feelings.

In the 1960s a lot of the drug use on college campuses was an attempt to find God or meaning through a drug-induced experience. Some religions teach that meaning comes from super-religious experiences apart from reason or our trying to understand or explain God or these experiences with words. Some religions even advocate drug-induced religious experiences. Unfortunately, some branches of Christianity have turned their backs on reason and teach people to seek only a succession of experiences to give them meaning or put them in touch with God.

For this reason, among others, Christians on many college campuses or in some churches find a lot of the teaching to be unreasonable and confusing, not to mention antibiblical. The teaching is unreasonable and confusing simply because it is irrational; *it really is unreasonable and confusing!* Rather than thinking he is ignorant and the teacher or preacher is "so intellectual," as he so often does in these situations, the Christian should be grateful that his life and teachings are built on a different foundation from those he is listening to, from those who have given up finding God or any meaning by the use of their reason or from the revelation of a God who speaks reasonably. Christians think differently from those who have given up finding God or any meaning by the use of their reason or from the revelation of a God who speaks reasonably. Christians think differently from those who have given up their use of reason as a means of understanding God and the world they live in. Turning to the irrational is only a sign of man's despair at seeking meaning through his reason *only.* Despair is a sign of the loss of all hope or confidence in man *himself,* of his ever finding the true God through his reason alone.

At the point of discovering that their reason is inadequate, people could have returned to the God of the Bible, and to the Bible's answer for their failure. But choosing to continue in their rebellion and with a desire to be autonomous from God, they moved instead to irrational thinking and to living on the basis of their feelings or experiences.

The second possible answer is at the opposite extreme from the first: People do not find God or meaning for living, because the fall so affected man's ability to reason that his reason is now dead or a zero. Therefore, it now takes "a streak of lightning," completely apart from reason, to convince man that God exists and that there is a meaning for life.

Some Christians who hold this view have really embraced an irrational perspective. There is very little difference between the person who bases faith on only a "zap" from the Holy Spirit apart from first understanding the objective, verbalized truth of the Bible, and the atheistic existentialist who bases his faith or "reason for living" on some "first-order experience"—an experience he cannot even talk about on the basis of reason. Both types of people are irrational. Why bother to talk reasonably and lovingly with a non-Christian, if you believe that only a "zap" from God is going to make him a Christian! Why bother to teach the non-Christian anything about Christ the Savior, when prayer for a "zap" is needed before he can understand *anything?*

Only an objective, historical revelation from God (the Bible), that we can reason about, can give us the basis for judging whether or not we have been "zapped" by God, by reality, or by the devil. We cannot wait to be "zapped" before we begin to reason about the Christian faith or take the claims of Christ seriously. The Bible, and not our experiences, must be our supreme authority in religious matters. When the memory of a "zap" fades away, we are able to think through again and again the reason for our hope, and we can be led back to a stable faith. If we believe that only a "zap" from God will make a person find God, then our basis for using reason to help people find God is eroded along with our efforts to do evangelism.

The Bible really teaches a third answer to man's situation and his capabilities. The Bible's answer is really somewhere between the two opposite extremes: Man will not find God and meaning by using reason *alone*. Neither will he find and know God *apart from the use of his reason*. The Bible approaches fallen man on the basis that even with his reason as it is now, God has given him good and sufficient reasons to bow and acknowledge that he is there. If man will not bow and acknowledge that there is a God, based upon the evidence all around him, then he is guilty before him. At the same time, God's grace and Holy Spirit are at work, but not in some mechanical way.

We must bow twice before God. First, we must bow and acknowledge that God is our Creator. We must acknowledge that we are his creatures. We are not and cannot be autonomous and independent of him, because he has created us—we are finite human beings under his Lordship and rule. Second, we must bow and acknowledge that we are guilty before God; we have sinned. We need him to save us from our sins and the results of our rebellion. As fallen man, and with the capacities we have now, we are held accountable by God if we do not bow twice.

Our problem with God is not metaphysical, in the sense that God is so big and we are so small that we cannot know him—in the sense that he is infinite and we are finite. Our problem is not with the way he made us. Our problem with God is a moral problem, in the sense that we have knowingly rebelled against God and have done things he has said we should not do. Our problem in this world is, too many people think they can live apart from a relationship with the God who is there and apart from the rules for living God has revealed in the Bible. Too many people do not realize that "God's rules for living" are for our own good, as well as for the good of the whole creation. His rules, like the owner's manual for a new automobile, are according to the way he designed us as unique individuals made in his image, and he also designed us to live with him and others in loving relationships.

Dr. Schaeffer says that when we become Christians, "We must bow twice, both metaphysically and morally." We must recognize who God is, who we are, and what we have become; this is to bow *metaphysically.* We must also recognize we are sinners before a Holy God and we need a savior: this is to bow *morally.* The world as it is and man as he is should convince anyone that God exists, but each person must choose to bow both metaphysically and morally.

Even though I am fallen, I still have authority (under God) to rule the earth and the things of the earth. But because I have sinned, I rule unwisely. I am worthwhile, but when I am in rebellion against God, my actions destroy not only myself but also those around me. I need a savior so I can rule this earth and work with others with wise compassion.

I have died spiritually. I am going to die physically, unless Christ comes again before I die. I will be eternally separated from God—die eternally—because of my rebellion, unless something is done. To overcome death in all these areas, I need a savior. Only God can be and provide that savior. This world is fallen and imperfect; it needs a savior too, and only the God who made it can provide that savior.

My problem is not simply lack of knowledge and the need to bow twice before God. If this were my only problem, I could bow twice now and be my own savior. I have sinned against a holy and significant God, and the sentence of death is upon me. Apart from God's action (free grace) I will always be dead spiritually. Apart from

God's grace, I cannot rule without my efforts bringing forth ashes.

What has God done about our need for a savior? What has he done and what does he intend to do to bring about life for those under the sentence of death? Is there a possibility of our ever ruling wisely, justly, and compassionately? Will there ever be a time when things will be good and right again? Will this earth always be subject to destructive tornados, earthquakes, floods, moths, mosquitoes, rust, and mildew?

13
GOD HAS A PLAN

WHEN ADAM AND EVE willfully chose to disobey God, they died spiritually. God had warned them this would happen if they disobeyed him. Their spiritual death came about *automatically,* before God ever discussed the matter with them. Their spiritual death manifested itself first in their feelings of guilt. Guilt, real guilt and guilt feelings, follows disobedience, and God created us to suffer guilt feelings automatically whenever we are really guilty.

Of course today, since the fall of man, we know that continual disobedience can dull guilt feelings while the guilt remains, and not all guilt feelings are related to real guilt or objective rebellion and disobedience. But Adam and Eve suffered real guilt and guilt feelings when they acted contrary to God's revealed will for their lives.

We know they died spiritually and suffered guilt because they tried to cover their nakedness with the clothing they made from fig leaves. They tried to hide themselves from each other. Their spiritual death affected their personal relationship. And when they heard

God "walking in the garden," they tried to hide their guilt and shame from him by hiding themselves from him. This seems like an unreasonable action to us, to think that you can hide yourself from the infinite God, but rebellion is unreasonable and brings forth continued foolish actions. When Adam and Eve rebelled, definite psychological consequences ensued, and their reason was impaired. They separated themselves from each other. Their rebellion made them try further to separate themselves from God. We see the same things today.

But the horrible consequences of spiritual death and eventual physical death would not be the end of it all. God would begin his restoration project with the very first ones in rebellion! He shared with Adam and Eve a part of his plan for redeeming the whole human race, even when he meted out a part of their punishment by excluding them from the garden and by bringing a curse upon the ground. Henceforth, the ground would be hard to tend and would bring forth weeds.

Like Adam and Eve, every one of us deserves the judgment of physical and eternal death. Every one of us who takes time to think things through has experienced or is experiencing spiritual death, the feeling of being separated from God and other persons. Every one of us has sinned, and every one of us has been a rebel in God's Kingdom.

But God has provided a way for us to approach him, and we need not face him only and always from the position of knowing and feeling our shame and guilt. God loves us and shows us his love, but at the same time he does not overlook our sin. God is holy, and if he just winked at our sins, there would be no moral absolutes. At the point of God himself, and at the point of his relationship with us and the world, everything would be relative. He must act in love and holiness while holding justice and mercy in the balance. He must uphold moral absolutes because he is the Governor of the universe, and he made the universe to operate according to both physical and moral laws that could not be broken, apart from certain consequences also taking place. We act upon this basis in the physical world every day, but fail to see the truth of the matter in our moral relations as well.

God began to reveal his solution to man's problem when he told Adam and Eve they had sinned and would be punished. But at the same time, he said there was also love and the possibility of forgiveness and restoration. The absolute remains, but there is mercy too—a mercy that does not overlook the seriousness of the crime.

God told Adam and Eve they could not solve the problem of the fall by themselves; they could not cover their guilt and shame by the works of their own hands. God took one of their friends, probably a little lamb, and killed it to provide skins to cover their nakedness. He demonstrated that sin was serious, and at the same time he pointed them to the future when a Redeemer would come from the seed of the woman. Woman, who had sinned first, would bring forth the Redeemer of the world! What a message of grace!

When God shed the blood of their innocent little friend, the lamb, right before their eyes Adam and Eve were shown that a substitution could be made for them. They would not need to suffer immediate physical death, because the death of the lamb was substituted for their death. Only in this way could God show the seriousness of their sin and the seriousness of his love for them at the same time. His action pointed them, without giving them all of the details, to the Lamb who would come, to God's only begotten Son, who would die on a cross as a substitute for the sins of the world.

God must have told Adam and Eve how he wanted them to worship in the future. He wanted them to sacrifice a lamb to remind them that their approach to him must always be *through faith* in him and in his just, righteous, holy, loving, merciful character and actions. Faith was to be the basis for their relationship, and holy living would flow from their faith.

No doubt Abel understood this when he sacrificed his lamb, but Cain went before God and brought his own works from his field. Cain came to God in an unacceptable way, and the Epistle to the Hebrews says Abel believed God and Cain did not. Cain did not approach God in faith. He further compounded his problem by bringing about the first physical death of a fellow human being, when he killed his own brother!

The sacrificial system which we find in the Old Testament pointed the people to the coming of the promised Redeemer. Throughout the Old Testament, God defined who this Redeemer would be, so that he would be recognized when he came. The Redeemer who would come and die would be a special Person who could be recognized upon the basis of all of the prophecies God would give in the course of the Old Testament history.

God spoke into history. As he spoke to the whole nation of Israel, he did so in a historically verifiable manner by showing them at the same time his strong arm in freeing them from slavery in Egypt. When God sent the Redeemer in the future, he would come in history in such a way that the people could verify who he was on the basis of what God had said in the past. God chose to be reasonable in his approach to solving man's problems, because he had made man in his image with the ability to reason. Even with the fall, man's reason was not so impaired that he could not study these things and understand the reasonableness of all that God would do to bring him salvation through faith.

Throughout the Old Testament we find that a small number of people had faith that God would send his Redeemer. They believed in God's promises and they acted on those promises. Before Christ actually came in the flesh and died, Abraham was saved through faith and not by works. King David was saved by his faith. These saints of the Old Testament were saved through their faith in the Christ who would come, and we are saved through our faith in the Christ who has come.

Before and after the coming of Christ, salvation has always been by grace through faith. No man can boast in the presence of our holy God, and no man can earn his salvation on the basis of his works. All of us have sinned, and the only way to God is now on the basis of what he has done. But can we see this evidence in the Old Testament? Can we see how Jesus Christ was the Redeemer to come?

14
GOD'S PLAN UNFOLDS

GOD PROMISED Adam and Eve that in the future he would send into the world a Redeemer for the whole human race. The Old Testament records many prophecies regarding his coming and whom the people should expect. The Redeemer came, and he was called the "Messiah" or "Christ" (which means the Anointed One or King). The prophets said he was to have certain characteristics that would prove he was the one God had promised to send to save his people from their sins.

We should be amazed when we think of the consistency of the Bible's teachings regarding the qualities of the coming Redeemer and the aspects of his coming. The Bible was written over centuries of time and by several different writers. The beautiful wholeness and consistency of the Bible's total teaching should tell us something about the Author's perfection. Surely he would give a perfect revelation to man as well as provide a perfect redemption of man.

God said the Redeemer would be born of a woman, of the seed of a woman and not of a man. When we remember that Jesus was born of a virgin, which means he did not have an earthly father, we understand the "hint" God gave about the promised Redeemer in Genesis 3:15.

If we could have thought ahead, we should have concluded that the Christ could only be born of one particular race of people and of one particular nationality; that is, if he was really going to be born of a woman. His one human parent could not just be mankind in general, but would obviously be of a particular race and nationality. It is reasonable for us to believe that God would reveal to mankind not only his race and nationality before he came, but further narrow this down for people to think about as they evaluated the claims of those who would claim to be the Christ, the Redeemer.

In fact, we find that God did this in the Bible. The Bible reports that God chose the Semitic peoples to be the ancestors of the Christ. This choice was narrowed down again to one particular family of the Semitic peoples. God appeared to Abraham and told him the Messiah would come through his line; one of his descendants would be the Redeemer. This family, of course, became the Jews.

The three most prominent ancestors of the Jews were Abraham, Isaac, and Jacob, called the "patriarchs." Jacob had twelve sons, and of these twelve God said the Redeemer would be born from the tribe of Judah. God later said the Redeemer would come from the royal line (or family) of King David, and he would be an eternal King.

The Sunday before his death, Jesus entered Jerusalem to proclaim that he was the King who was to come. He accepted the people's praise of him and told the religious leaders that if the people were silent, even the stones would cry out! When he was on trial before Pilate, he told him plainly that he was a King, but that his Kingdom was not of this world.

Christ is King in three ways. As Creator/God he is the King or Ruler over all things. All people will see this some day, and all people will bow before him when he comes again. Since he is the King of the universe, and since he will come again to make known to all people that he is indeed this special King, we have the privilege of making him the King of our lives personally, moment by moment, now.

According to the Old Testament, not only would the Redeemer be a King from the family of Israel's greatest king, David, but he would also be a Prophet. He would speak for God to man. He would demonstrate not only how we should live by his actions, but by his actions he would demonstrate the character of God. The Old Testament told the Jews to look for a prophet greater than Moses. The Prophet/Redeemer would give true knowledge, propositional knowledge to mankind (knowledge that is true to reality, but not exhaustive knowledge). As a Prophet he would reveal more about the nature and character of the Trinity than had been revealed prior to his coming. He still gives us knowledge through the Holy Spirit, but this knowledge will always be consistent with the Bible, if it is really from him.

In addition to being a King and a Prophet, he would also be a Priest. A priest is one who intercedes between God and man in the conducting of worship and in prayer. The role of the prophet was to tell man how to live, and call him to responsibility. The king would make the laws, enforce the rules, and be the chief administrator of the kingdom. And the priest would intercede between God and man on man's behalf, whenever man disobeyed God and repented of his sins.

Only those from the tribe of Levi could be priests, because God did not want the roles of king and priest to be united in one person until the Redeemer came. Prior to the coming of the Redeemer, God wanted separation of powers. Perhaps the leaders of the Reformation practiced this procedure to some extent because of God's practical way of handling the affairs of state in the Old Testament times. God did not want the monarchy and the priesthood united in one person until the Messiah could do this perfectly and safely.

We are told in the Bible how the Messiah could qualify to be a Priest, even though he could not be both from the family of Levi and the family of Judah. He would be of the order of Melchizedek, as the Epistle to the Hebrews in the New Testament would later demonstrate.

Because we are sinners, we need more than the knowledge a prophet can bring. We need forgiveness and holiness. As our Priest, Christ removes the guilt of our sin from us and gives us the opportunity to live holy lives once again. Christ was different from the high priest in the Old Testament. He did not need to offer a sacrifice for his own sins, because he was perfect and without sin. Since he is also the infinite/personal God, no other sacrifice for sins will ever be needed again; his sacrifice has infinite value. As High Priest, he did not offer the blood of a lamb to God, but he offered his own blood as *the* Lamb of God.

Jesus fulfilled all these roles of King, Prophet, and Priest to demonstrate to the people that he was the Redeemer.

Jesus would not only fulfill these roles of high rank,

but he would also come as a servant and live as a servant upon the earth. Born into the family of a lowly carpenter, he was born in a stable in Bethlehem, the city the Scriptures foretold. He washed his own disciples' feet. And then, as the suffering Servant foretold by the prophet Isaiah in chapter 53 and by King David in Psalm 22, he would hang on a cross and die a cruel death to enable his Father God to be both just and loving when he forgave sins. Jesus was the Law-maker, but he would die for the Law-breaker. As Priest, he would sacrifice his own life as the Lamb of God for the forgiveness of sins. He would die, but then he would be raised again and live forever as the High Priest of heaven. There he presents our case before the throne of justice whenever we sin and repent. We are to strive not to sin; when we think about the great sacrifice of our Redeemer in our behalf, we have further motive not to sin, but when we do sin we have a Defender, Jesus Christ, who speaks in our defense as the great High Priest.

From the Bible, we learn that Jesus was more than a man. He was born of a woman; God was his Father, and God called him his Son. Jesus claimed to be God when he walked upon this earth. Only as both God and man would Jesus Christ do all of the things he had to do in the different roles placed upon him, and do them perfectly.

We recognize that Jesus claimed to be God when we look at several of his claims about himself. Jesus claimed to have the authority to forgive sins—not just sins against himself as a fellow human being, but sins against God himself, and only God can do that! Before he ascended into heaven, following his resurrection, he gave a command to his disciples that included the statement that he would be with them always, throughout all time.

Earlier he had said that wherever two or three met in his name, he would be there. In these statements he was claiming the ability to be everywhere at one and the same time for all time. Only God can do that and he does so by his very nature as the infinite God. Jesus told his listeners that he was living before Abraham was born. He claimed that God his Father loved him before anything was created! As noncreated and in relationship with his Father before anything was created, Jesus was claiming to be the personal God. We have seen in preceding chapters the importance of the infinite/personal God as far as philosophy and theology are concerned. In the Bible we find that Jesus Christ, a real person (human being) of history, claimed to be the Second Person of the Trinity, the infinite/personal God.

Jesus fulfilled various human and governmental roles upon this earth after he was born of Mary. As God and man, he died as our substitute to save us. And then he sent his Holy Spirit, the Third Person of the Trinity, to indwell us, guide us, and pray for us when we cannot pray for ourselves.

15
THE EMPTY HANDS OF FAITH

KNOWLEDGE *alone* of the God who is there, knowledge of the infinite/personal God, the Father, Son, and Holy Spirit, will not solve all of our problems or save us from our sins. But when we learn who he is, we should bow to him. If we do not, we are guilty of disobedience.

When we learn who he is, another problem arises; we also learn that we have sinned against a God who cares. God cares about us personally. He cares about how we live, and he cares about whether we sin or not. God cares about how we treat ourselves, other people, and our world. What we do matters to the infinite/personal God who is there. And he is always acting to show everyone how much he cares.

On the one hand, knowing that God is there is an encouraging hope and it gives us a reason to carry on in this world. But on the other hand, it brings us under guilt and condemnation, because we have destroyed so much that could have been so beautiful, and God cares about that. Is there a solution to the problem of knowing God and at the same time knowing that we are sinners and deserve his punishment?

How can we be rescued from our sins and the separation sin brings between ourselves and God? Only God can solve the problem, and that is why he sent Jesus Christ to be our Redeemer, our Savior. Jesus Christ brought salvation, and a part of salvation is imparting true knowledge, but that is not the totality of salvation.

We are saved by grace; grace means "free gift." God was gracious when he did not immediately destroy Adam and Eve for their rebellion. His "free gift" to them was continued life and fellowship with him through the blood of the lamb. When God sent his only begotten Son, Jesus Christ, into the world, Jesus Christ was another one of his "free gifts" for the whole human race.

Once we understand who God is and the "free gift" of his Son, who died in our behalf so that we could be forgiven, we need to receive this "free gift." We are saved from our sins when we receive with the empty hands of faith God's free offer of salvation in Jesus Christ. "Salvation is obtained by faith in Christ, plus nothing." We are saved by grace through faith; we are not saved by any humanistic works of our own. We cannot earn God's free gift of forgiveness; all we can do is "receive the gift."

When we understand how reasonable and just are God's requirements or "laws," then we must face the fact that we have been wrong before God. When we look at our lives and analyze our behavior even apart from knowing God, we must also admit that we have not even kept our own ideas of right and wrong. We have required others to live up to certain standards of our own making, but when we are honest with ourselves we have to admit that we haven't even kept our own man-created "rules for living." We have not kept God's laws or our own laws. When we face the judgment, we *might* be able to plead that we did not know God's laws, but if we do, God will be able to show us how we broke our own standards. We will stand guilty before him!

From his first promise to send a Savior, God went to elaborate efforts to help people come to the conclusion that they should accept Jesus Christ as their Savior, as a "free gift" of his love. We have seen something of these elaborate efforts in the Old Testament prophecies and in the life and ministry of Jesus himself, as King, Prophet, Priest, and Servant. If there were any other way of salvation for rebellious mankind, God would have used it. The salvation of mankind depended upon the death of his Son. The Bible says there is only one way of salvation, and Jesus said he was "the Way." A condition of receiving salvation is receiving Jesus Christ as Savior.

If we do not accept Jesus Christ as our Savior, then we have rejected God's "free gift" of forgiveness. If we reject God's free offer of forgiveness, then we are choosing to remain under God's judgment. "For God so loved the world that he gave his one and only Son, that whoever believes in him shall not perish but have eternal life" (John 3:16).

If we choose to reject salvation, then we are also choosing all the consequences that God has promised us in judgment. We will not be able to justify our rejection of Christ when we meet him at the judgment seat in heaven. Only Christ will be able to justify our admittance into God's presence, but his justification of our salvation will be not upon the basis of our works. He will justify our salvation upon the basis of his sacrifice for our sins and upon our having received him and that sacrifice for us through faith.

God can be just when he forgives us, because Christ

died in substitution for our eternal death. His death in our behalf removes our moral guilt when we receive him in faith. As far as God is concerned, we are cleansed from all sin. Just as God has forgiven us and even forgotten our sins, when we accept Christ as our Savior, so we should accept our forgiveness and forget our past sins to the point of not bearing about an unnecessary load of guilt.

Because Christ perfectly kept the law of God, his death could be in our behalf as a condition of our salvation, based upon the love of God. Once we are justified by Christ (and we are justified when we accept him as our Savior), we have peace with God. It is just as though we had never sinned! We are no longer at war against him or at war with ourselves. We should know this is true because God has declared it to be true in the Bible, but it should also be a matter of our personal experience with God.

God has never overlooked sin, because he is a holy God. Out of his infinite love, he has always made the effort to forgive us and restore us to a personal relationship with himself.

We know that Moses and Elijah appeared with Jesus on the Mount of Transfiguration and they talked about his death upon the cross. God had forgiven them of their sins, and he had received them into paradise, but upon the conditions of *the future death of his Son* and *their faith in his future coming.* Perhaps Moses and Elijah were speaking to Jesus about the importance of his death for the sins of the world, as well as for their own sins. What an encouragement this conversation would be to Jesus upon the Mount of Olives; he could remember it as he prayed right before his betrayal, trial, and condemnation. Jesus knew he had to die to satisfy the claims of justice, so he submitted his will perfectly to the perfect will of his Father. God in his great wisdom and love was able to devise a plan to forgive sinners and still be just in doing so. That plan included the death of his Son. What a wonderful love he must have for us!

In one sense, Christianity is the easiest religion, because Christ has done it all. He offers us the free gift of salvation, and we only have to receive our forgiveness. But in another sense, Christianity is the hardest religion. We cannot be accepted by God on the basis of any of our works, because we are sinners, and in the past we have been rebels in the Kingdom of God. To be saved, a person must bow before the God who is there, and give him his loyalty; he must submit as a loyal subject to the Governor of the universe. A person must bow twice, recognizing who God is and his own dependence upon God because he is fallen and a sinner. People in their stubborn pride want to live independently from God, and even though they know the facts and the sure consequences of continued rebellion, they may still choose not to bow.

16
WELCOME TO YOUR NEW FAMILY

WHEN WE RECEIVE Jesus Christ as our personal Savior, we are received into God's family. God becomes our Father, and Jesus Christ becomes our Brother.

Before we become Christians, we are people created by God in his image, but we are not members of his family. Christians are *adopted* into God's family through Jesus Christ. We are not God's children until we come to him through faith in Jesus Christ. We cannot be his children prior to becoming Christians, because we are separated from God by our rebellion and our true moral guilt. For this reason Jesus could look at some of the religious leaders of his day and declare, "I know who your father is; your father is the devil!" Jesus calls us to leave the kingdom of darkness, Satan's family, and enter the kingdom of light, God's family. When we become Christians, we do so because we have chosen to leave one family and join another.

Our new relationship with God is characterized by a new, prayerful relationship with him. We can call him "Father" in the same personal sense that Jesus used when he prayed "Abba," which means "Daddy." We can run to our Father at any time, no matter what the need or problem, in the same way that any child should be able to run into the loving arms of his or her earthly parents. When we pray the Lord's Prayer, we recognize that God is our Father, but we also pray that his name be reverenced. We can come to God as our Daddy, but we must also come with respect, the same respect we should be able to give to our earthly father. When we pray the Lord's Prayer, we are also recognizing that God is the King of the universe and that we want to obey his will. So when we pray, we should approach the King of the universe as his dearly beloved child, but at the same time we should go to him with respect for him, respect for his Kingdom and to do his will.

As God's children we know that we still have much to learn as members of his family. Sometimes we disobey our heavenly Father, and this should grieve us immediately, even as it brings much sorrow to him. We should go to our Father immediately and tell him we are sorry and do not intend to do such a thing again! If we persist in our disobedience, then God will bring appropriate and necessary discipline to us in the situation. Because we are his beloved children, he does not give us up, but seeks through many means to restore us to right fellowship in his family. Sometimes we will do things or fail to do things from lack of knowledge, and as our Father, God will do what is necessary to direct us in the way that we should go. This guidance includes sending the Holy Spirit to indwell us, but it also includes his arranging circumstances to teach us lessons, and sometimes (for our own good) these lessons are accompanied by pain. But in all things, there is no better father than our heavenly Father. Many who have not had good earthly fathers learn for the first time, when they become members of God's family, what a good father is through their new relationship with their heavenly Father.

"Being saved" does not just mean that your sins are forgiven so you can go to heaven. Salvation in your life includes what God has done in the past for you, when Jesus died on the cross; it includes what God is doing for you in the present as a member of his family; and it includes much much more that he will do for you and also for the whole universe after Christ comes again. He will completely restore all things. Salvation is a total work of God. Salvation is not just "getting saved."

When we become Christians, our salvation not only includes admittance into God's family, but it includes a new ongoing relationship with God's Son, Jesus Christ. The Bible teaches that we are "united with Christ," and through some of his parables, Jesus told his disciples what this would mean. The Bible sometimes describes our identity with Christ as being "in Christ." And Christ himself prays for us to have a real unity with him.

When we become Christians, we are united with Christ, and Christ begins to live in us. Before we became Christians, Jesus was calling us to accept him as our Savior, and the Father was drawing us toward him. But when we actually yield ourselves to Christ as Savior, he will come into us and live within us. Not enough Christians realize what a difference this should make in their lives, in the things they should stop doing and in the things they should start doing! When we become Christians, we involve Christ personally in everything we do, and many times we grieve Christ and the Holy Spirit by the things we say and do!

Jesus describes our union with him by using another aspect of family. Our union with him is described as a marriage. He is the groom and we are the bride. Just as Scripture teaches that a husband and wife become "one flesh," so the believer has this close union with Jesus Christ. But just as the husband and wife do not lose their individual identities in this oneness, neither Christ nor we lose our individual personalities in our union with him. There is real unity, but a unity that respects the integrity of each person concerned.

Preserving the integrity of the individual in union with God is completely absent in most Eastern thought. In becoming "One" (united) with "Brahman" (the name of the highest Hindu god), the individual loses not only his identity but his consciousness as well. He becomes so absorbed in the god that he completely disappears. For these reasons, among others, prayer in most Eastern thought is a meditation technique that voids the mind of all conscious thought. The goal is an empty mind, because in Eastern meditation there is no conscious god to talk to, and the Eastern god is certainly not conscious of the believer's existence. This philosophical pantheism is so hard to live with that the Eastern religions have created millions of gods to solve their problem with it and try to satisfy their longing for a personal relationship with a god.

We need to emphasize that union with Christ is unique from other religions. It means we can have the closest conscious, personal relationship with God that is possible without violating who God is or who we are.

In marriage, children are often born to their parents. Likewise, when we are married to Christ we should cooperate with him so he can bring forth spiritual children who will become members of God's family. Through his indwelling, we should bring forth much fruit for him. We should set our minds on doing his will and being faithful in our marriage to him.

In addition to speaking about our union with him as a marriage, Christ said he is the vine and we are the branches. Our spiritual life depends upon his life flowing through us. If we keep our lives in touch with him, consciously asking him to bear his fruit in our words and actions, then we will be able to do much for him. Our efforts in union with him will bring forth lasting results, in his name, in him, and in his wisdom, love, and power. We must recognize our weakness and personal inadequacies as his servants, but this should not drive us to despair. Rather, truly seeing how limited we are in ourselves should drive us to him, not for salvation only, but so his strength can work in us in spite of our weaknesses.

When we become members of God's family, not only is Christ our Brother, but we become related to brothers and sisters all over the world! There is a new "Brotherhood of believers" that the Bible calls "the communion of the saints." There is no "universal fatherhood of God" or "universal brotherhood of man." Yet, every person should know some crucial things: 1. God has created each of us in his image. All of us are alike in "kind"; we are all members of the human race. 2. Every living person is my neighbor, and I should treat him equally with myself. 3. If I truly love my neighbor, I should do what I can to help him become a member of God's family.

As a member of God's family I have the privilege of sharing with my brothers and sisters in Christ in three different areas. My relationship with others should make a practical difference. When you enter God's family, and join a Bible-believing church, you should find that believers share spiritual help, material help, and enjoy fellowship and companionship with one another. Being a member of God's family brings us blessings in our vertical relationship with God as well as blessings in our horizontal relationships with fellow believers in Jesus Christ.

Dr. Schaeffer tells us:

> If we have accepted Christ as our Savior, we have the responsibility to search out a Bible-believing group of God's people, where there is right doctrine and real community in love, and meet with them. We should not join ourselves to just any group that calls itself Christian, but one where the teaching is truly biblical, where discipline is maintained concerning life and doctrine, and where there is true community. If there is *no* such group geographically available (and there are such places), then prayerfully before the Lord we should find even a small number to meet for worship, prayer, study, encouraging one another, and to have community.[1]

1. *Basic Bible Studies,* in *The Complete Works,* Volume Two, p. 358.

17
SPECIAL BLESSINGS

WHEN JESUS CHRIST was born into our world, he came to fulfill some very special responsibilities. The Old Testament prophets spoke of the coming Redeemer. They said he would serve as a King, a Priest, and a Prophet, among other roles.

After Jesus Christ rose from the dead, he told his followers that they too would have some very important privileges and responsibilities to fulfill. Later the Apostle Peter would declare the nature of these blessings and privileges very concisely: "But you are a chosen people, a royal priesthood, a holy nation, a people belonging to God, that you may declare the praises of him who called you out of darkness into his wonderful light" (1 Peter 2:9).

As we have shown, Jesus Christ came into the world to be our High Priest, to save sinners. He still serves as our High Priest. He has chosen us to serve as priests in this world. Each of us who has received Jesus Christ as Savior has the privilege of praying directly to God in Jesus Christ. We are united with him, and he is our High

Priest; through him we are admitted into the very presence of God himself. We need no other intercessor in our behalf than Jesus Christ himself, and we should exercise the privilege of going to God directly in prayer and of receiving the blessings from that very special relationship that we can have. As a priest of God, we have the privilege of interceding in prayer for the lost. We have the privilege of pointing people to the God who is there. Just as Jesus sacrificed himself in our behalf, while we were still sinners, we should be willing to sacrifice ourselves that people might come to know Jesus Christ as their High Priest and accept his sacrifice for their sins.

Jesus Christ is the prophet who was greater than Moses. We are united with Christ if we have received him as our Savior and Lord. If we have fellowship with him, we too are prophets. Christ came into the world to give the world true knowledge about God and reality—not exhaustive knowledge, but true knowledge nonetheless. We have true knowledge from him that must be shared with the rest of the world. This true knowledge has been recorded in the Bible. We have the personal blessings which come from this true knowledge, and we have the privilege of sharing this knowledge with others so they too can enjoy the blessings we enjoy. Not only do we have the privilege of being prophets in Jesus Christ, we have the moral obligation to be prophets! Our world and our culture are dying and people are lost without any meaning for life or continued living. We do not love our neighbors as ourselves if we are unwilling to share with them the message of a total salvation. Sometimes we rationalize, saying, "Well, everyone I know is a member of a church." If so, we still have the obligation to talk with them about their faith, and help them if certain aspects of their faith are not according to the true knowledge we have from the Bible. The prophets of the Old Testament spoke not only to kings and princes, but also to the people and to the leaders of the established Jewish religion (church). We have the same obligation.

Jesus Christ is King of the universe. In the future, when Christ comes again, Christians will rule with him on this earth. Our life now is a training ground to prepare us to rule wisely, justly, and compassionately. We are not going to be prepared to rule then if we are not consciously trying to rely now upon the leadership of Christ our King in all our personal and governmental relationships. Some Christians have the privilege of great responsibilities now, of great power and authority over others. They should serve in these roles as Christ the King would serve and under his daily direction. If all of us try to live responsibly under his Lordship now, we will be prepared to rule wisely wherever he chooses to place us in his coming visible Kingdom upon this earth.

We have the great privilege, in Christ, of serving as priests, prophets, and kings. But we have other privileges and blessings as well. The Bible says we are a living temple, and that the Holy Spirit indwells the Christian. The Third Person of the Trinity indwells us when we accept Christ as our Savior. As God, when the Holy Spirit comes to indwell us, so the Father and the Son come to indwell us as well. When we approach God in prayer, we approach the God who is there in heaven, and also the God who is indwelling us. For this reason, he understands us and our needs far better than we do. For this reason, the Holy Spirit can intercede for us with sighs that words cannot express when we are unable to pray for ourselves (Romans 8:26).

With this great blessing of the Holy Spirit's indwelling us come certain other consequences. The Holy Spirit condemns the sin of the world. If we are living as consistent Christians, our ways of life will confront the world with its sin, and the world will react to us. Sometimes the world will seek to persecute us as it persecuted him; at other times people will be moved to repentance and faith.

The work of the Holy Spirit includes leading the nonbeliever to faith in Christ, to repentance, and to obedience. The Holy Spirit points people to Christ and to his work. The Holy Spirit wants our active cooperation in the task of leading people to salvation through faith in Jesus Christ. The Holy Spirit wants to build up the Church with people who are living stones, and he wants the Church to make certain that Jesus Christ is the cornerstone of the building. The Holy Spirit will help the Church interpret and apply the Word of God in its life, and he will guide the individual as well. Through the indwelling Holy Spirit we can say with the Apostle Paul, "I can do everything through him who gives me strength" (Philippians 4:13).

18
TRUE SPIRITUALITY

DR. SCHAEFFER called "sanctification" "true spirituality." His understanding of true spirituality was developed in the early 1950s, and I have dealt with it at length in the first portion of this book, "The Man."[1]

As we have noted, salvation is a total work dealing with the past, the present, and the future. Salvation past, present, and future is based upon the finished work of Christ when he died on the cross in substitution for us.

The theological term "justification" relates to the work of Christ in the past, as his death made possible God's just forgiveness of our sins. We are "justified" when we become Christians, accepting Christ as our Lord and Savior.

The theological term "sanctification" relates to the work of Christ in the present, but it is a work based upon his work of justification in the past. Sanctification is a process of cleansing that should go on in the life of the believer as his relationship with Christ as living Lord and Savior is further developed. True spirituality is living differently after we have been justified. True spirituality is bearing spiritual fruit through the work of the indwelling Christ.

When we become Christians, the moral law of God does not become unimportant. The moral law of God is an expression of the character of God, and since God's character will never change, the moral law will never change. Furthermore, the moral law describes how we should live, based upon how we are made. God's moral law is a rule for human and *humane* life. We are saved by grace through faith, and not by good works based upon the moral law or otherwise. "But after we are saved, we should show forth our gratitude in our lives by good works."[2]

As Christians, we know that if we die we will live again. Jesus promised us he was going to heaven to prepare a place for us. The Bible also teaches that Christians will receive rewards in heaven, and these rewards will be based upon the good works we have done following our becoming Christians. Even after we become Christians, God gives us incentive to keep on keeping on. Our work in his behalf and for his Kingdom will receive appropriate rewards. Still, even as Christians, our "good works" should not be humanistic in the sense of relying on ourselves or on our own strength. Our "good works" must be the works we perform in the strength, power, grace, and love of the Holy Spirit. Our "good works" must be the "good fruit" that God bears through us as we seek to be obedient to him.

We must set the same standard for our lives that God sets. Jesus commanded, "Be perfect, therefore, as your heavenly Father is perfect" (Matthew 5:48). Yet, if we sin and confess our sins, as Christians, God is faithful and just to forgive us our sins, and cleanse us from all unrighteousness (1 John 1:9). But we are presumptuous to think that we can go on committing the same sins over and over, and confessing the same sins over and over, and that God will not do anything about this unfaithfulness!

Jesus Christ is not only a savior from the punishment of sin. The Bible teaches that Jesus "will save his people from their sins" (Matthew 1:21). The indwelling Christ will work with his cleansing power in our lives as we turn to him for the power to overcome sin and sinful habits. We must decide to let Christ Jesus reign in our lives in opposition to the power of sin. As we turn our lives over to him completely, moment by moment, we should have true spirituality flow forth from our lives.

Sanctification is a process that begins when a person accepts Christ as his Savior and Lord. It is a way of living, based upon the total meaning of the finished work of Christ in our lives moment by moment. We cannot be perfect apart from Christ's being our Savior from sin at every moment. We must put our faith in him and in his power at every moment, or else we are living in disbelief of the total work Christ wants to do in our lives.

True spirituality is based upon our developing relationship with the Lord Jesus Christ. God has given us means of grace for developing this relationship. We can know Christ more personally through the study of the Bible. Christ is revealed in the Bible in the varied and many ways that he wants to have a relationship with us as a Savior from our sins. We can pray directly to Christ, and the more we converse with Christ, the better we will get to know him and his power to save us from sin. We can ask the Holy Spirit to teach us better the meaning of the Bible teachings, and we can ask Christ to deliver us from temptation. As we are obedient to Christ day by day, we are strengthened in our relationship with him, and as we tell others about his saving grace, we have greater fellowship with him as he bears his testimony through us. Finally, we are strengthened as we rely upon the fellowship God wants us to have with fellow believers. Our fellow believers will be able to comfort us with the same comfort they received in times of trials, troubles, and temptations.

If we are practicing any sin, we are doing so because we have not asked Christ to be our Savior from that sin, and we have not applied to that sin the many means of grace Christ has provided for us. True spirituality includes allowing Jesus Christ to be a total Savior in our present lives.

1. Dr. Schaeffer's fine treatment of the subject of sanctification is *True Spirituality* in *The Complete Works,* Volume Three, "A Christian View of Spirituality," Book Two.

2. *Basic Bible Studies* in *The Complete Works,* p. 360.

19

THE RESTORATION OF ALL THINGS

THE BIBLE TEACHES a complete system of thought from beginning to end, from "in the beginning God" to the creation of the universe—including the creation of man in God's image—to the fall of man, to God's plan of salvation, and then to the complete restoration of all things.

When we are justified by grace through faith, God declares we are forgiven. Sanctification is the manner in which God works in our lives in this present world. But another theological term is "glorification." The Christian experiences glorification at his death, and in the future we will see the complete restoration of all creation.

We will die a physical death, unless Christ comes back before we die. If we are Christians, when we die our body will return to the dust of the ground, but our soul will go immediately to be with Christ in paradise. Jesus gave this promise to the thief who repented on the cross. Christ indwells us, and as Christians we are the temple of the Trinity in a personal relationship with the God who is there. At the Christian's death, the indwelling Christ takes him or her to be with him in heaven.

The soul will leave the body at death and go to be with Christ, while the body returns to the ground. But this is an unnatural situation. God created man body and soul, and God said the body and soul were good. God does not intend for us to live for eternity as disembodied spirits. Hence, the real significance of Jesus' bodily resurrection becomes clear. Jesus Christ rose, body and soul, from the dead, and his body was a glorified body, a glorified human body. Just as Christ was raised from the dead with a glorified human body, so at some point in the future our souls will be reunited with our glorified human bodies. Those bodies will be substantially the same as the bodies God gave to Adam and Eve before the fall. How much difference there will be between our bodies and theirs is not worth speculation, but when our bodies are restored to us, then our salvation is complete. God originally made us as whole people, and redemption restores us to being whole people.

If Christ comes again before we die, then the bodies of both the living and the dead will be glorified in an instant. These bodies will be like Christ's body after his resurrection, and Christ took great effort to show his disciples that he indeed had a glorified, real human body following his resurrection. His body could pass through doors and he could eat, and we will be able to do the same in our glorified bodies.

In addition to the restoration of our bodies and souls, if we are Christians, God intends in the future to restore both heaven and earth. Our world as it is will not get better, because it is a fallen world. Our hope is not that the world will get better; our hope is the second coming of Christ. Our hope is in the final defeat of Satan and

God's restoration of the heavens as well as the earth. But this does not excuse us from working to reform and renew our culture and society, as well as the church!

We know from the Scriptures that the future is secure for the Christian, and the Christian will rule with Christ when his salvation is completed. But there will also be a future resurrection for those who have died while in rebellion against God. The lost will face condemnation at the final judgment, because with all the evidence of God's great love for them all around them, they chose instead to continue a life of selfish rebellion. Dr. Schaeffer gives this stern warning: "Either a person must be twice-born (natural birth and the new birth when he takes Christ as Savior), or he must die twice (the natural death and eternal judgment)."[1] And in conclusion he says:

> If we are Christians, in the light of this study we should give ourselves to the task which Christ has given to the Church in this age—telling others the content of the gospel.
>
> If you have not yet taken Christ as your Savior, if you are not a Christian, the triune God invites you to come and accept God's free gift of salvation by accepting Christ as Savior.[2]

1. *Basic Bible Studies,* p. 370.
2. Ibid., p. 370.

20
HOW TO BECOME A CHRISTIAN

WHEN THE SCHAEFFERS began L'Abri, they did so for the purpose of being able to give honest answers to honest questions. They sought to give honest intellectual answers to the problems of modern men and women, but they wanted their answers to be based upon the teaching of the Scriptures. They proved that it is possible for a Christian to be true to the clear teachings of Scripture and maintain intellectual integrity at the same time.

The Schaeffers also recognized the importance of demonstrating the truth of their beliefs by the way they lived. The most hardened skeptic would be challenged to investigate the truth of the Christian faith by the Schaeffers' demonstration in their way of life of the existence of the God who is there: Father, Son, and Holy Spirit. By their keeping these two aspects of their work in balance, they have helped many thousands become Christians as the direct result of their ministry, and Christians around the world have seen the importance of this balanced approach in sharing the claims of the gospel.

Edith Schaeffer has described their work in her book *L'Abri,* and those who have joined the Schaeffers over the years in the work of L'Abri have done so for a reason that certainly relates to their approach to the Christian faith:

> There are those who have become Christians, not through a leap of faith on the basis of emotionalism, but on the basis of certainty in the area of logical answers to the real questions which are at the root of the too-often surface considerations. Then, on the basis of making a choice in a given moment of history, they have submitted to the God who is there. They have a burning desire to communicate the truth of the universe and the existence of God in the medium of their own talents.[1]

In the previous chapters of this book you have been given good and sufficient reasons (in spite of my own imperfections) to bow before the God who is really there and accept Jesus Christ as your Lord and Savior. If you do not bow, you are guilty before him, and your continuing rebellion will have certain dire results.

In the early days of L'Abri, the Schaeffers used what they called "The Four Questions" to help a person measure himself to see where he stood in relation to God. In these four areas you can rethink the claims of the Christian "good news" regarding salvation. As you think through these four areas, God will expect you to make a choice about whether or not you will believe in him or call him a liar.

The Schaeffers emphasized consistently that each person's response to the good news makes an eternal difference: "Man has been given free choice from the beginning. He is not a puppet, and no one will force him to believe, or act upon anything he does not want to. However, consequences of his belief and actions are set forth. The choice is always his."[2]

"As a man thinketh, so is he." If you are not a Christian, or if you do not know whether or not you are a Bible-believing Christian, you need to make some personal decisions in these four areas.

1. DO YOU BELIEVE GOD EXISTS?

You cannot become a Christian unless you believe God exists. God is truly, objectively there. We have seen that people hold different views of God. You cannot become a Christian unless you believe that the God of the Bible really exists. The God of the Bible is the infinite/personal God who is three persons: Father, Son, and Holy Spirit. God is holy and just. God is Love and Truth. God is Spirit. God is eternal: Father, Son, and Holy Spirit have no beginning and no end. They are uncreated. They have always existed. The three persons of the Trinity have always loved each other and been in fellowship. For this reason we have an explanation for personality in the universe and for why *we* have personality and a need for fellowship with our Creator and our fellow human beings.

Edith has written: "When we say you must believe in the existence of God, it is the *God of the Bible* we are talking about, not the God of some human being's definition: whether defined in wood, stone, and gold as a material image, or defined in words as an image of the imagination."[3]

2. DO YOU ACKNOWLEDGE THE FACT THAT YOU ARE A SINNER, AND THAT YOU CANNOT GET RID OF THIS GUILT BY YOURSELF?

In the preceding chapters we have seen that sin is rebellion against God, and it involves disbelieving the Word of God. If we have ever disobeyed God once, we are objectively guilty before him. We have not even obeyed the standards that we have set for ourselves and others, let alone God's perfect standard. God has simply commanded us to love him and love our neighbors as ourselves, and we must recognize that on many occasions we have chosen not to do this. Indeed, when we are in rebellion against God, we are placing self-love above love for God and neighbor; therefore, our disobedience is destructive of very important relationships. We may not have any psychological guilt "feelings," but we do have true moral guilt. We must recognize our need to get rid of our guilt and overcome our sin. This leads us to consider what the Bible says about Jesus.

3. DO YOU BELIEVE THAT JESUS CAME, IN SPACE, IN TIME, AND IN HISTORY?

Do you believe what the Bible teaches about Jesus? Do you believe he was born of a virgin and God was his Father? Do you believe he lived a perfect and sinless life? Do you believe he died upon the cross in substitutionary atonement for us? Do you believe he physically rose again on the third day? Do you believe he appeared to his followers and commanded them to be his witnesses throughout the world? Do you believe he then ascended into heaven and will come back a second time? These are crucial areas of belief about Christ, if you are going to be saved and be a Bible-believing Christian. But Edith Schaeffer has warned us about stopping at just these three areas:

> This is the third area. . . . It's true that a person can believe these first three "areas" of fact with his intellect, and yet not really be a Christian. The fourth question or area involves *bowing to this God, and accepting what Christ did as for you, personally and individually, taking your deserved punishment, for your individual sins, as He died outside Jerusalem.*[4]

4. WILL YOU BOW BEFORE GOD, AND ACCEPT JESUS CHRIST AS YOUR PERSONAL LORD AND SAVIOR?

We have shown that Jesus Christ is God and that he sacrificed himself for us because of his great love for us. He cares about each of us personally, and he is extending his forgiveness to all people on the condition that they will receive him and his atoning death. Will you bow before him, and follow him as your Lord and Savior?

Salvation is "not a matter of grabbing on to a bunch of slogans, nor of having merely an emotional experience . . . It is for good and sufficient reasons *believing* these things are true, and then making a definite decision to accept, and say, 'Thank you' to God for it."[5]

1. *L'Abri,* p. 224.
2. Ibid., p. 181.
3. Ibid., p. 164.
4. Ibid., pp. 165, 166.
5. Ibid., p. 166.

APPENDIX

"AND GOD RAISED US UP WITH CHRIST AND SEATED US WITH HIM IN THE HEAVENLY REALMS IN CHRIST JESUS, IN ORDER THAT IN THE COMING AGES HE MIGHT SHOW THE INCOMPARABLE RICHES OF HIS GRACE, EXPRESSED IN HIS KINDNESS TO US IN CHRIST JESUS. FOR IT IS BY GRACE YOU HAVE BEEN SAVED, THROUGH FAITH—NOT BY WORKS SO THAT NO ONE CAN BOAST. FOR WE ARE GOD'S WORKMANSHIP, CREATED IN CHRIST JESUS TO DO GOOD WORKS, WHICH GOD PREPARED IN ADVANCE FOR US TO DO." EPHESIANS 2:6-10

A
CHRONOLOGY OF THE LIFE OF FRANCIS AUGUST SCHAEFFER IV (1912-1984)

1912 Born on January 30 in Germantown, Pennsylvania. The only child of Francis August Schaeffer III, and Bessie Williamson Schaeffer.

1914 On November 3, his future wife, Edith Rachel Merritt Seville, born in China. The fourth child of George Hugh Seville and Jessie Maude Merritt Seville.

1930 Became a Christian after reading the Bible, beginning with Genesis.

1931 In September, entered the freshman class at Hampden-Sydney College in Virginia.

1932 On June 26, met his future wife at the First Presbyterian Church in Germantown, Pennsylvania.

1935 Graduated second in his senior class, magna cum laude, with a B.A. degree from Hampden-Sydney College. On July 26, married Edith, and in September entered Westminster Theological Seminary in Philadelphia, Pennsylvania.

1936 After learning that Dr. J. Gresham Machen had been defrocked, left the Northern Presbyterian Church, and joined the Presbyterian Church of America.

1937 In the summer, helped with the founding of Faith Seminary in Wilmington, Delaware, after a split from Westminster. On June 18, Priscilla born.

1938 Following graduation, the first pastor ordained in the

Bible Presbyterian Church; began ministry as pastor of the Covenant Presbyterian Church in Grove City, Pennsylvania.

1941 Moderator of the Great Lakes Presbytery of the Bible Presbyterian Church; and on May 28, Susan born in Grove City, Pennsylvania; became associate pastor of the Bible Presbyterian Church in Chester, Pennsylvania.

1943 Became the pastor of the Bible Presbyterian Church in St. Louis.

1945 On May 3, Deborah Ann born in St. Louis, Missouri.

1947 Toured Europe for three months in the summer as "The American Secretary, Foreign Relations Department, of the American Council of Christian Churches" and as a board member of the Independent Board for Presbyterian Foreign Missions.

1948 The family met Dr. C. Everett Koop at the Philadelphia Children's Hospital, while Fran served as moderator of the Bible Presbyterian Church in Nashville, Tennessee. The whole family went to be missionaries in Europe, living in Lausanne, Switzerland. Fran helped with the formation of the International Council of Christian Churches.

1949 Moved to Chalet des Frenes in Champery, Switzerland, and wrote *Basic Bible Studies.*

1950 Spoke at the Second Plenary Congress of the International Council of Christian Churches, after visiting Karl Barth in his home.

1951 Walked in the hayloft of Chalet Bijou in Champery to rethink his Christian convictions. After experiencing a personal revival, began an emphasis on sanctification and the work of the Holy Spirit, laying the foundation for the book *True Spirituality.*

1952 On August 3, Francis August Schaeffer V born in Champery, Switzerland.

1953 In May, the family returned to America on furlough.

1954 On May 28, awarded the honorary Doctor of Divinity degree by Highland College. In September, returned to Switzerland.

1955 On April 1, moved to Chalet les Mélèzes in Huémoz. On June 5, resigned from mission board and began L'Abri Fellowship.

1958 The foundation for English L'Abri laid with speaking engagements in England.

1960 Ranald Macaulay helped found Farel House study center at L'Abri.

1968 The first L'Abri Conference held at the Ashburnham conference grounds in England. His first books published.

1971 On June 12, received the honorary Doctor of Letters degree from Gordon College.

1972 Toured universities around the world.

1974 Spoke at the Lausanne Congress on World Evangelization. Began work with his son on the book and film: *How Should We Then Live?*

1977 In January, 5,600 people attended the first seminar for *How Should We Then Live?* Helped found the Council on Biblical Inerrancy. Began work with Dr. Koop and Franky on *Whatever Happened to the Human Race?*

1978 In October, diagnosed to have cancer at Mayo Clinic in Rochester, Minnesota.

1979 In January, the film series *How Should We Then Live?* shown in Rochester with Dr. Schaeffer leading discussion in the midst of chemotherapy treatments. In June, held L'Abri Conference in Rochester with almost 2,000 people attending. In September, began the first seminars for *Whatever Happened to the Human Race?* L'Abri moved its American headquarters to Rochester, Minnesota.

1982 Published *The Complete Works of Francis A. Schaeffer, A Christian Worldview* in five volumes.

1983 Received the honorary Doctor of Laws degree from the Simon Greenleaf School of Law.

1984 Completed *The Great Evangelical Disaster* and seminar tour. Died on May 15 at his home in Rochester, Minnesota. Funeral held on May 20 in the John Marshall High School Auditorium with interment at Oakwood Cemetery in Rochester, Minnesota.

B
WHAT CAN WE LEARN FROM FRANCIS SCHAEFFER?
Larry E. Wilson

I can confidently predict that Dr. Francis A. Schaeffer (who died of cancer on May 15, 1984) will be remembered by future church historians as one of the most significant Christian leaders of the 20th century.

Dr. Schaeffer had a noteworthy ministry, influencing a numerous and broad spectrum of people. President Reagan eulogized, "He will long be remembered as one of the great Christian thinkers of our century, with a childlike faith and a profound compassion toward others. It can rarely be said of an individual that his life touched many others and affected them for the better; it will be said of Dr. Francis Schaeffer that his life touched millions of souls and brought them to the truth of their Creator."

Countless disenchanted youth found new life and hope in the historical Christian faith through the work of Dr. Schaeffer. Further, as Stephen Board commented in *Christianity Today* (June 15, 1984), " . . . he enjoyed unusual credibility among most American evangelicals and many fundamentalists."

This is particularly remarkable when it is recognized that Dr. Schaeffer was Presbyterian and Reformed (i.e., Calvinistic!). Dr. Schaeffer often alluded to this by referring to himself as "a man of the Reformation," by speaking of and citing John Calvin with favor, by lauding the fruits of the Reformation in

Western culture and the influence of the Puritans in early America, and by praying and working for *"reformation* and revival" in our day.

How could Francis Schaeffer, as a Reformed Presbyterian, attain the broad-ranging influence that he did? Of course, his brilliance as an analytical thinker and his copious and "swash-buckling" style as a writer were critical factors, but I think there is a deeper, more foundational reason.

I think Dr. Schaeffer embodied an exemplary balance between what has been called "pie, doc, and kuyp" tendencies among Christians. Many Christian leaders have tended, I believe, to emphasize one or two of these perspectives to the exclusion of the others(s). "Pie," or pietists, emphasize personal devotion to the Lord, personal evangelism, prayer, etc. "Docs," or doctrinalists, stress biblical teaching, theological accuracy, church purity, etc. Finally, "kuyps," or Kuyperians, dwell on social and cultural involvement, Christian approaches to philosophy, art, economics, politics, etc. Unhappily, Christians have tended to polarize over these differing emphases. Balanced Christianity, on the other hand, would encompass all three emphases. To my mind, Dr. Schaeffer embodied that balance—in his life, in his ministry, and in his writings.

In his final book Dr. Schaeffer described the overarching commitment that drew these perspectives into an integrated whole:

> Throughout my work there is a common unifying theme which I would define as "the Lordship of Christ in the totality of life." If Christ is indeed Lord, He must be Lord of all of life—in spiritual matters of course, but just as much across the whole spectrum of life, including intellectual matters and the areas of culture, law, and government. I would want to emphasize from beginning to end throughout my work the importance of evangelism (helping men and women come to know Christ as Savior), the need to walk daily with the Lord, to study God's Word, to live a life of prayer, and show forth the love, compassion, and holiness of our Lord. But we must emphasize equally and at the same time the need to live this out in every area of culture and society.

It was this balance, I think, that gave Dr. Schaeffer credibility across such a broad spectrum of people. Christians from differing perspectives saw that he shared and promoted their concerns.

It was also this balance that made Dr. Schaeffer one of the most significant Christian leaders of the 20th century. With his wide-ranging credibility, Dr. Schaeffer was able to lead many believers (including our Christian leaders) to broaden their horizons and transcend their own truncated "pie, doc, or kuyp" emphases. The impact of this trend is still being felt. It is strengthening the Church's witness to the world, for there is an increasing concern to minister to whole persons with a whole Christianity. It is also helping the Church internally, for as Christians see the value of those emphases which they have been neglecting, they are beginning to recognize that other Christians have already cultivated those particular strengths. But above all, it is bringing glory to our God, and that was Dr. Schaeffer's burning desire all along.

What then can we learn from Francis Schaeffer? Of course, we can learn all sorts of particulars, but I think the greatest lesson is deeper. We may even disagree with certain particulars, but let us not allow that to blind us to the lesson we so need to learn in our day. Let us learn from Dr. Schaeffer the lesson of balanced Christianity—that we must become "pie-doc-kuyps"! Let us learn from Dr. Schaeffer the lesson of "the Lordship of Christ in the totality of life"! Let us learn from Dr. Schaeffer the lesson of the power of live Reformed orthodoxy!

This article first appeared in *Presbyterian Journal,* October 3, 1984, and is reprinted here by permission of the author.

C
L'ABRI TODAY

L'Abri is a living memorial to Francis Schaeffer. L'Abri is not just tapes, books, films, and buildings—as impressive as these are in themselves. L'Abri is Christian people, individuals and families, who together comprise a larger family that tries to demonstrate the Lordship of our Savior Jesus Christ over the whole of life.

When money was sent to the Schaeffer family to be used in memory of Dr. Schaeffer, it was given by them to L'Abri to carry on his work among people around the world.[1] L'Abri helps people become Christians so they can join the family of our heavenly Father. L'Abri also reaches out to show that God's message to man should make a difference in every human endeavor.

Every person who is what he is today because of the direct or indirect influence of Francis Schaeffer is a living memorial to him. Insofar as every person touched by him remains loyal to Jesus Christ, he honors his memory.

Every one of Dr. Schaeffer's children is in some form of vital Christian endeavor. Dr. Schaeffer was concerned about the testimony that Christian parents make to their children, so that their children might not turn away from Christ because of their Christian parents' imbalance in their work. He tried hard to be a fine father to his biological children, as well as a spiritual father to them and others. The fact that every one of his children is so active and competent in Christian work says something for his commitment to them individually, to his family, and to the idea of the Christian family, even in the midst of the trying Christian work that L'Abri was and continues to be over the years. Dr. Schaeffer's children and grandchildren are a memorial to him in the sense that they know Christ and bear him witness, whether they remain in L'Abri or not. How much better it is to make our memory live in the redeemed lives of people, than feel we must leave just a number of biological offspring in the world to carry on our name. The larger L'Abri family too is now made up of the spiritual children and grandchildren of those who became Christians through its ministry.

Having been involved in the life of Rochester L'Abri from its beginning, having attended L'Abri Seminars and Conferences, and having evaluated both Huémoz and Gryon L'Abri personally in August of 1984, I believe important observations should be made about the work of L'Abri around the world today.

First, I am impressed with all of the L'Abri leaders and teachers I know and have heard. I think that at one time or another I have met personally and visited with L'Abri members and workers from every branch. In every case, the L'Abri leaders and teachers I have met are totally committed to Jesus Christ as their personal Lord and Savior. They are intelligent, competent, compassionate, and on the cutting edge of what concerns people, or should concern people today. They are not just rehashing old ideas or restating Dr. Schaeffer's positions as though he had written infallible creeds. L'Abri leaders and teachers are informed about current events and ideas, and they bring God's inerrant Word to bear upon the world as it is today. L'Abri has gotten bigger, but it has not become impersonal or mechanical. People can still arrive at L'Abri and be warmly welcomed and guided to a solution of their problems under the Lordship of Jesus Christ and according to his Word.

L'Abri is not perfect; those who work there and those who have been to various branches have their own perceptions of

L'Abri's imperfections. Perhaps too many now sit around the tables. Perhaps the meals are too long and the days are too organized for an extended period of study during the day. Perhaps different branches have lacked organization at different times. Perhaps the staff has been too busy to see each person individually for as long as that person felt he needed to visit. But whatever the individual observations and complaints, the work of L'Abri has been so substantial and consistent in its work over the last thirty years that we can praise the God who is there for his wonderful grace in its life and work.

During my visit to Switzerland, I was impressed that Ranald and Susan Macaulay, along with their family, would leave England after twenty years and go to Huémoz, making a radical uprooting and replanting. Ranald and Susan, living in Chalet les Mélèzes, the first home of L'Abri, bring a stability and teaching capacity that makes a significant difference in the life of anyone who studies there and commits himself to learning what Huémoz L'Abri has to offer.

In Gryon L'Abri, Udo and Debby Middelmann have the unique intelligence and ability to communicate the relevance of the Christian faith as it relates to the needs of the Third World. Debby has a sound understanding of the dangers that utopian answers for our problems will bring us, and Udo's traveling around the world on behalf of Food for the Hungry brings him unique insight into the dangers of a Marxist interpretation of Christianity and enables him to teach the biblical interpretation of Christianity in light of the current social policies of many churches and governments. L'Abri will carry on beautifully under the Lordship of Christ because of Francis and Edith Schaeffer's faithfulness to L'Abri, and because of L'Abri's faithfulness to God and his leading.

It would be presumptuous of me to think I could describe every detail of every branch of L'Abri around the world today, especially since I have not been to every one of them. The great variety, individual creativity, and trials of the people in L'Abri can best be seen in their own words. And for this reason, Edith Schaeffer writes a "L'Abri Family Letter" several times each year. You may request placement on the "L'Abri

Family Letter" mailing list by writing: L'Abri Fellowship, 215 15th Avenue, S. W., Rochester, Minnesota 55902. You may also visit L'Abri for study, tape listening, or discussions at the following branches:

HUÉMOZ L'ABRI
Address: Chalet les Mélèzes, 1861 Huémoz, Switzerland.
Home of Ranald and Susan (Schaeffer) Macaulay and John and Priscilla (Schaeffer) Sandri, among many others. Larry Snyder is the co-ordinator of Huémoz L'Abri. Many of those mentioned in the books *L'Abri* and *The Tapestry* are still doing ministry there. Of great significance is the very recent acquisition of Chalet Bellevue for study and use by the handicapped, among others.

GRYON L'ABRI
Address: Chalet les Montaux, 1882 Gryon, Switzerland.
Home of Udo and Debby (Schaeffer) Middelmann.

DUTCH L'ABRI
Address: Kromme Niewe Gracht 90, 3512 HM Utrecht, Holland.
Home of Wim and Greta Rietkerk. You may write Anky Rookmaaker at this address.

SWEDISH L'ABRI
Address: Per Staffan and Lisa Johansson, Ryggasstugan Ransvik, N. Strandvagen 72, 260 42 Molle, Sweden.
Home of Staffan and Lisa Johansson.

ENGLISH L'ABRI
Address: The Manor House, Greatham, Hampshire, GU33, 6HF, United Kingdom.
Home of Jerram and Vicki Barrs, Barry and Veronica Seagren, Richard and Jane Winters, Cissie Sights, and Millie Thompson.

ROCHESTER L'ABRI
Address: L'Abri Fellowship, 215 15th Avenue, S.W., Rochester, Minnesota, 55902
Home of Edith Schaeffer, Julie Cooper, Ann Brown, Greg and Mary Jane Grooms, Jim and Gail Ingram.

SOUTHBOROUGH L'ABRI
Address: L'Abri Fellowship, 49 Lynbrook Road, Southborough, Massachussetts 01772
Home of Dick and Mardi Keyes, Susan McNab, and David and Darby Zink.

1. See Mike Yaconelli, "A Not So Fitting Memorial," *The Wittenburg Door,* No. 78, April-May 1984, pp. 31, 32.

D
THE WORKS OF L'ABRI

This concluding section, listing the books, tapes, and films, by Dr. Schaeffer, has been kindly provided by Richard W. Cook of Sound Word Associates. Up-to-date catalogues with current prices and tapes of the most recent L'Abri Conferences can be ordered directly from Sound Word Associates, P. O. Box 2035, 430 Boyd Circle, Michigan City, Indiana 46360. The following pages are taken from "L'Abri Cassettes, Catalogue No. 5."

AN INTRODUCTION TO L'ABRI

"If you continue in my words . . . you will know the truth, and the truth will make you free," John 8:31, 32.

Some have supposed that L'Abri is "only for the intellectuals." This has never been the case and is not the case today. A wide range of people visit Greatham L'Abri and the other L'Abri centers. Our conviction is simply this: the Bible is true. Three things flow out of this:

1. Because the Bible is authored by God, it is completely reliable and free of mistakes in whatever it says, whether in the area of theology, morals, history, or science. The Bible is both objective and demonstrable truth. Christians have

been hesitant about the "intellectual" side of their faith. This is remarkable in view of the clear position of the Bible at this point. Paul said all people were without excuse, that is, intellectually, in failing to acknowledge the evidence of creation (Rom. 1:18). He also described his ministry as "destroying arguments and every proud obstacle to the knowledge of God, and taking every thought captive to obey Christ" (2 Cor. 10:5). From Acts we know this included reasoning with people, trying to persuade them of the truth. In doing this he was not being a rationalist. He was merely living out his conviction that Christianity is really true and therefore demonstrable. Therefore, far from having to apologize for our faith we should have the same confidence Paul had when he said to Festus, "I am not mad, but I speak words of truth and sound sense" (Greek—"rationality," Acts 26:25).

2. The truths found in the Bible are relevant to all of human experience. The Bible speaks to every area of human activity and cannot be limited to what 20th-century man calls "religion." While the Bible identifies the central problem of man as the moral one of sin and judgment, and this must always be kept central in any Christian teaching, it also says things that are relevant to all other spheres of human interest and study, such as history, art, psychology, education, and politics, without being a textbook on any one of them. Therefore, you will see that the material in this catalogue is wide ranging.

3. Because the Bible is objectively true, it is true for all types of people, so there is the possibility of speaking both to those who have had considerable exposure to the thinking of our day, for example in colleges and universities, and also to those who have had little. The material in the cassettes includes both simple and also more complicated teaching.

So behind the material is the conviction that the Bible is true. "True" not just in terms of teaching, or of ideas for the mind, but "true" for the business of life itself. Alongside the material, therefore, it must be remembered that we are attempting in the residential centers to give some demonstration, albeit poor, of the fact that the words of the Bible, when accepted and acted upon, do lead to freedom and life. We hope, therefore, that the material in the catalogue will be viewed in such a context with no one cassette considered in isolation. The catalogue should be viewed as a unit.

CONTENTS

KEY TO NOTES (Appearing Alongside Tape Titles)

(A) If you are unfamiliar with or bewildered by all this material, these lectures are suggested as a beginning.

(B) Consult the book list. This material, by the same author, may be covered by a book and may be cheaper, more convenient, and more comprehensive that way.

(X) Poor quality recording or editing, or an incomplete series. These are a collection, having been recorded under various conditions in different countries over a long period of time. All are included because they are considered valuable; some are included despite their technical shortcomings because of the exceptionally good content.

Short passages of music in some of the music lectures are of execrable recording quality but serve their purpose usefully as illustrations. In all cases tapes may be returned and expenses will be refunded if you are dissatisfied.

(J) These tapes are available translated into Japanese.

L'ABRI CASSETTES BY FRANCIS SCHAEFFER

APOLOGETICS: THE DEFENSE OF BIBLICAL CHRISTIANITY

Christian Apologetics (X) 13.2
Apologetics is concerned with the defense or justification of a particular position. Dr. Schaeffer's argument for historical biblical Christianity. This tape ends abruptly.

Possible Answers to the Basic Philosophical Questions (B) 1.1a, 1.1b (Two tapes)
Describes and contrasts the possible answers to the problem of existence and man's moral dilemma.

Epistemology: The Early Wittgenstein (B) 11.2a, 11.2b (Two tapes)
Why the Christian does not have a problem in epistemology and the Christian's unity of external and internal reality.

Basic Problems We Face (B) 43.4, 45.1 (Two tapes)
Part 1, the problem exposed, the Christian communicates in the area of Truth as opposed to contentless religious experience. Part 2 gives examples.

Intellectual Proof and Faith (A) 8.1
The Christian life is based on both knowing and believing God. Intellectual proofs alone are not sufficient.

Exclusive Christ in an Inclusive Age 39.4
The necessary exclusion of paganism, the Judaizers and modern eclecticism.

The Christians and Our Moment in History 157.3
In order to communicate to our generation and in order not to be infiltrated by it, we need to know two things: (1) What

Christianity is in contrast to what it is not. (2) To understand the form which the world spirit has at our point in history.

ANALYSIS OF MODERN THOUGHT

The Development of Modern Thought (B) (13 tapes)

14.1 Introduction: Two roots of Berkeley 1964—Aquinas to the Renaissance
14.2 Aquinas to the Renaissance, continued. How the Reformation stood against this
14.3 Development of modern science
14.4 Shift from modern science to "modern-modern" science
14.5 The shift in philosophy: Rousseau, Kant, Hegel, Kierkegaard
14.6 The spread into other disciplines: art, music, general culture, theology
14.7 The new theology and the results of higher criticism
14.8 The spread geographically and by classes. The forms of existentialism
16.1 Contemporary results of Berkeley 1964: monolithic culture, rebellion, films. Introduction to cosmogony
16.2 Cosmogony, limits to possible answers
16.3 More on Christian cosmogony. What comes next in society with the loss of absolutes: hedonism, 51% majority, elites
16.4 What is coming, majority in society, elites
16.5 What is needed to speak to our age: two contents—two realities

The Change in the Concept of Law in the U.S.A. 95.2, 95.3 (Two tapes)

Relativism in the 20th Century 1.2a, 1.2b, 1.2c, 1.2d (Four tapes)
A description of the relativism of our century as exhibited in economics, morals (Kinsey), politics, Protestant and Roman Catholic theology. The historian Toynbee discussed.

Practical Results of the Death of Absolutes (B) 52.3a, 52.3b (Two tapes)
Morality for the relativist—an invalidation of the message of

the Swiss painter, Paul Robert, concerning the Reformation basis of law (Justice pointing to the Bible) has very practical results in the area of morals. (An abrupt beginning.)

Chance and Evolution 12.1a, 12.1b, 12.2a, 12.2b (Four tapes)
Darwin's personal dilemma after accepting an evolutionary view of the world; Arther Koestler's advocacy of a chemical solution to man's divided self; Michael Polanyi's refutation of reductionism in a review of his essay "Life's Irreducible Structure."

Authoritarian Government 8.2
What lies ahead for the Christian, followed by questions and answers on government manipulation and conflict between civil law and biblical absolutes.

Neo-orthodoxy 32.3
Based on an article in *Prism*. Shows how neo-orthodoxy is a new form of the old liberalism.

The Modernity of Fundamentalism 53.2a, 53.2b (Two tapes)
Review of John Opie's article in the *Christian Century*. Crucial area of epistemology is examined.

Vatican Council II 19.2, 19.3a, 19.3b, 20.1a, 20.1b (Five tapes)
This was given before and while the Council was in session. The tensions in the Roman Catholic Church and a discussion of its view of individualism as contrasted with that of the Reformation.

Peter Versus the Papacy 75.4
Is there any biblical basis for the Roman Catholic doctrine of Peter's primacy?

India from 2600 B.C. to 1800 B.C. 31.3a, 31.3b (Two tapes)
An historical investigation. Why did the Aryans who moved into India develop a pantheistic, experimental type of religion whereas the other Aryan groups did not?

Difficulties in the Way of Mutual Appreciation of Eastern and Western Spiritual Values and Suggestions on How to Overcome Them 35.2a, 35.2b (Two tapes)
A review of Dr. H. H. Presler's article in the *India Culture's*

Quarterly. The similarity between the liberal theology of the West and the spiritual values of the East, contrasted with historical Christianity.

"How Sanskrit and Hindi Relate to Hinduism" 35.1
A review of Presler's article in the *I.C.Q.* The relationship between a language and the cultural thought which produced it, with reference to linguistic analysis and Christian communication.

Eastern Thinking In Western Theology 33.3
Pointing out the similarities between the spiritual values of the East and the modern neo-orthodox theology of the West. Based on Presler's article in the *I.C.Q.*

THE BIBLE: ITS NATURE AND OUR APPROACH

Five Problems of Those Who Deny the Evaluation of the Bible Regarding Itself 29.1a, 29.1b, 29.2, 29.3, 31.1 (Five tapes)
(1) The archaeological problem of Albright. (2) The literary problem of E. Auerback. (3) The technical or statistical problem, computer analysis. (4) The legal problem, the use of the higher critical method in the plagiarism case against H. G. Wells. (5) The problem of religious authority, the inspiration of Scripture and the claims of Jesus. The practical problems with knowledge, prayer, and action for those who deny the Bible's claims for itself.

Inspiration of Scripture 13.1
How our presuppositions affect our view of inspiration.

Freedom and Limitation in Biblical Cosmogony 8.3
A consideration of the early chapters of Genesis and the limits of interpretation in this crucial section of the Bible.

The Problem of Dating the Early Chapters of Genesis 25.2a, 25.2b (Two tapes)
Is the cultural situation described in Genesis in conflict with archaeology? With reference to a paper read at Oxford by James O. Buswell III.

The Cultural Background of the Bible 46.3a, 46.3b, 44.2a, 44.2b (Four tapes)

The correlation between biblical history and contemporary secular history from 2000 B.C. to A.D. 80.

Prophecy 144.1 to 153.4
See under DOCTRINAL STUDIES. (Forty tapes)

Final Choices 115.3
Conclusions drawn from the film series *How Shall We Then Live?* A reaffirmation that the Bible speaks to us in matters of history and the physical world as well as in spiritual matters. An answer to criticism in David Winter's book *But This I CAN Believe.* (Most of this lecture is printed in a pamphlet "It Is Essential for the Truth of Christianity That the Bible Relates Truth about History and the Cosmos, As Well As about Spiritual Matters," available from Greatham.)

THE BIBLE: EXPOSITION

Job (Four tapes)
22.2 The problem and rationale of history
22.3 The problem of whether we live in a moral or amoral universe
22.4 The problem of suffering—is it always chastisement?
24.1 What was Job's mistake?

Ecclesiastes 33.1, 33.2a, 33.2b (Three tapes)
An exegesis, considering Solomon, Leonardo da Vinci, and the dilemma of modern man.

Daniel 45.2, 45.3a, 45.3b, 46.1, 46.2 (Five tapes)
A critical yet constructive examination of Driver's critique of Daniel, a liberal theologian's approach to prophecy.

Romans (A, X) (Twenty-three tapes altogether)
Chapters 1-8. In three parts.

1. JUSTIFICATION Introduction. Sin, guilt and man's need for salvation. Christ's work and justification by faith. (Ten tapes)

3.1	(Ch 1:1-15)	4.2	(Ch 2:24-3:31)
3.2a, 3.2b	(Ch 1:15-22)	4.3	(Ch 3:31-4:11)
3.3	(Ch 1:22-2:1)	5.1a, 5.1b	(Ch 4:11-5:1)
4.1a, 4.1b	(Ch 2:1-24)		

2. SANCTIFICATION Presents aspects of salvation. Law and grace. (Nine tapes)
   5.2a, 5.2b (Ch 5:1-10) 6.2 (Ch 7:1-25)
   5.3a, 5.3b (Ch 5:11-6:1) 6.3a, 6.3b (Ch 8:1-18)
   6.1a, 6.1b (Ch 6:1-23)
3. GLORIFICATION Future aspects of salvation. (Four tapes)
   7.2a, 7.2b (Ch 8:18-25) 7.3a, 7.3b (Ch 8:26-39)

DOCTRINAL STUDIES

Bible Doctrine 99.1 to 114.2 (63 tapes)

Prophecy 144.1 to 153.4 (40 tapes)

Revelation 133.1 to 143.3 (43 tapes)
These three series, "Biblical Doctrine," "Prophecy," and "Revelation" may be studied separately but were designed to be considered together as a course in theology. The total listening time for the entire course is about one hundred and fifty hours. "Biblical Doctrine" is a systematic analysis of the Westminster Confession of Faith and a copy of this should be obtained to study with. It divides into two main parts, the first on justification and the second on sanctification or "true spirituality." The "Prophecy" series examines the nature of prophecy in the Bible and establishes the principles of interpretation. These principles are then applied in the "Revelation" series. "Prophecy" and "Revelation" also appear under the heading THE BIBLE above.

It was felt that these three series would be of particular value to schools, seminaries, or other institutions as well as to individuals. The book *True Spirituality* completes the course as a detailed study of sanctification.

Absolute Limits of Christianity (A) 26.4
The limits of Christianity beyond which one no longer holds to true Christianity.

Illustration of Absolute Limits 25.3
Shows how pantheism is implied when it is taught that the final concept is a unity of energy between God and creation

as well as when held to be a concept of crude mass. Material from Salvador Dali, Teilhard de Chardin, and some true evangelicals who seem confused.

Before the Beginning 42.3
The necessary basis for healing in our alienation.

The Active Obedience of Christ 32.2

"The Shout of a King Is Among Them" 39.3
Do we listen to Christianity as merely a pleasant song or as truth which demands serious action?

"On the Problem of Evil and the God of Love" 82.1, 82.2 (Two tapes)
A discussion of an article by Professor John Hick, "The Listener."

CHRISTIANITY AND THE ARTS

Some Art Norms 11.1a, 11.1b (Two tapes)
Twelve criteria for the evaluation of art.

Art Forms and the Loss of "The Human"
10.1a, 10.1b (Two tapes) How modern art norms have been emphasized at the expense of humanness in art. Architecture, Rookmaaker's analysis of the elements of art, and material from Paul Klee.

10.2a, 10.2b (Two tapes) Analysis of the elements of art. Paul Klee's and L. Baskin's views compared with Rookmaaker's. Klee's "unconscious" elements in his paintings.

10.3a, 10.3b (Two tapes) L. Baskin's analysis of the irrational in modern art.

The Theatre of the Absurd 34.1a, 34.1b (Two tapes)
Review of M. Esselin's book. Introductory glances at de Sade, Simone de Beauvoir, Hemingway, Bergman, Fellini, le Carre, Andy Warhol, Francis Bacon. Postscript, showing how modern man is unable to live with absurdity.

THE CHRISTIAN LIFE: SPIRITUAL EXPERIENCE

Practical Christian Living 95.4

Impracticable Ethics 20.3
Love and forgiveness. Are Christ's teachings impracticable idealism in a fallen world?

Vindication of God, or Vindication of Self? 32.1
1 & 2 Samuel. The corruption of David's principle of non-self-vindication. The same things in our lives which are virtues when applied with God's law become evils when applied outside of it.

Murmuring 20.2
The implications for us of the cause and consequence of the Israelites' murmuring against God in the wilderness. (Ex. 15:24, 16:2, 17:3, etc.)

Three Young Men in the Furnace 32.4
Daniel 1-3, Hebrews 11. Faith and commitment to God, whether he delivers us or not.

THE CHRISTIAN LIFE: PRAYER, WORSHIP, AND THE CHURCH

Framework for Prayer 26.3
Orthodoxy as the only intellectual basis and motivation for prayer.

Prayer Series (Four tapes)
24.2 What is prayer?
24.3 Why we pray so little; power of prayer
26.1 Faith in prayer
26.2 Intensity and importunity in prayer

Thanksgiving 43.3
The importance of thankfulness in our personal and corporate worship and its relation to true spirituality. (See also "Psalm 73," 58.4.)

Little People, Little Places 128.3
Are there important and unimportant Christians in the Lord's work and are there important and unimportant places—or

does God give us another criterion for judgment of ourselves and others?

THE CHRISTIAN LIFE: MARRIAGE, SOCIETY, AND THE STATE

Christian Sex Ethic 21.1
Based on the Belgrade Ballet's performance of Joan de Karisse. A modern rendering of Don Juan.

The Christian and Government 157.4
What is a Christian's relationship to civil government, and is there a place for civil disobedience by the Christian?

The Christian and Revolution 53.3a, 53.3b (Two tapes)
Is revolution ever permissible? Based on Agatha Christie's book "Murder in the Calais Coach."

TITLE INDEX—BY PART NUMBER/BY AUTHOR

6.2 Romans Ch7/1-25
6.3a Romans Ch8/1-18 Tape 1 of 2
6.3b Romans Ch8/1-18 Tape 2 of 2
7.2a Romans Ch8/18-25 Tape 1 of 2
7.2b Romans Ch8/18-25 Tape 2 of 2
7.3a Romans Ch8/26-39 Tape 1 of 2
7.3b Romans Ch8/26-39 Tape 2 of 2
8.1 Intellectual Proof and Faith
8.2 Authoritarian Government
8.3 Freedom and Limitation in Biblical Cosmogony
10.1a Art Forms and the Loss of "the Human" Tape 1 of 6
10.1b Art Forms and the Loss of "the Human" Tape 2 of 6
10.2a Art Forms and the Loss of "the Human" Tape 3 of 6
10.2b Art Forms and the Loss of "the Human" Tape 4 of 6
10.3a Art Forms and the Loss of "the Human" Tape 5 of 6
10.3b Art Forms and the Loss of "the Human" Tape 6 of 6
11.1a Some Art Norms Tape 1 of 2
11.1b Some Art Norms Tape 2 of 2
11.2a Epistemology—The Early Wittgenstein Tape 1 of 2
11.2b Epistemology—The Early Wittgenstein Tape 2 of 2
12.1a Chance and Evolution Tape 1 of 4
12.1b Chance and Evolution Tape 2 of 4
12.2a Chance and Evolution Tape 3 of 4
12.2b Chance and Evolution Tape 4 of 4
13.1 The Inspiration of Scripture
13.2 Christian Apologetics
14.1 The Development of Modern Thought Tape 1 of 13
14.2 The Development of Modern Thought Tape 2 of 13
14.3 The Development of Modern Thought Tape 3 of 13
14.4 The Development of Modern Thought Tape 4 of 13
14.5 The Development of Modern Thought Tape 5 of 13
14.6 The Development of Modern Thought Tape 6 of 13
14.7 The Development of Modern Thought Tape 7 of 13
14.8 The Development of Modern Thought Tape 8 of 13
16.1 The Development of Modern Thought Tape 9 of 13
16.2 The Development of Modern Thought Tape 10 of 13
16.3 The Development of Modern Thought Tape 11 of 13
16.4 The Development of Modern Thought Tape 12 of 13
16.5 The Development of Modern Thought Tape 13 of 13

19.2 Vatican Council II Tape 1 of 5
19.3a Vatican Council II Tape 2 of 5
19.3b Vatican Council II Tape 3 of 5
20.1a Vatican Council II Tape 4 of 5
20.1b Vatican Council II Tape 5 of 5
20.2 Murmuring
20.3 Impractical Ethics
21.1 Christian Sex Ethic
22.2 Job Tape 1 of 4
22.3 Job Tape 2 of 4
22.4 Job Tape 3 of 4
24.1 Job Tape 4 of 4
24.2 Prayer Series Tape 1 of 4
24.3 Prayer Series Tape 2 of 4
25.2a Prblm Dating Early Chapters of Genesis Tape 1 of 2
25.2b Prblm Dating Early Chapters of Genesis Tape 2 of 2
25.3 Illustration of Absolute Limits
26.1 Prayer Series Tape 3 of 4
26.2 Prayer Series Tape 4 of 4
26.3 Framework for Prayer
26.4 Absolute Limits of Christianity
29.1a 5 Prblms in Dnying Eval of Bbl Rgrdng Itslf Tape 1 of 5
29.1b 5 Prblms in Dnying Eval of Bbl Rgrdng Itslf Tape 2 of 5
29.2 5 Prblms in Dnyng Eval of Bbl Rgrdng Itslf Tape 3 of 5
29.3 5 Prblms in Dnyng Eval of Bbl Rgrdng Itslf Tape 4 of 5
31.1 5 Prblms in Dnyng Eval of Bbl Rgrdng Itslf Tape 5 of 5
31.3a India from 2600 B.C. to 1800 B.C. Tape 1 of 2
31.3b India from 2600 B.C. to 1800 B.C. Tape 2 of 2
32.1 Vindication of God or Vindication of Self
32.2 The Active Obedience of Christ
32.3 Neo-orthodoxy
32.4 Three Young Men in the Furnace
33.1 Ecclesiastes Tape 1 of 3
33.2a Ecclesiastes Tape 2 of 3
33.2b Ecclesiastes Tape 3 of 3
33.3 Eastern Thinking in Western Theology
34.1a The Theatre of the Absurd Tape 1 of 2
34.1b The Theatre of the Absurd Tape 2 of 2

35.1 How Sanskrit & Hindi Relate to Hinduism
35.2a Dflclty in Apprctn of Estrn&Wstrn Sprtl Val Tape 1 of 2
35.2b Dflclty in Apprctn of Estrn&Wstrn Sprtl Val Tape 2 of 2
39.3 The Shout of a King Is Among Them
39.4 Exclusive Christ in an Inclusive Age
42.3 Before the Beginning
43.3 Thanksgiving—Psalm 73 (see 58.4)
43.4 Basic Problems We Face Tape 1 of 2
44.2a Cultural Background of the Bible Tape 3 of 4
44.2b Cultural Background of the Bible Tape 4 of 4
45.1 Basic Problems We Face Tape 2 of 2
45.2 Daniel Tape 1 of 5
45.3a Daniel Tape 2 of 5
45.3b Daniel Tape 3 of 5
46.1 Daniel Tape 4 of 5
46.2 Daniel Tape 5 of 5
46.3a Cultural Background of the Bible Tape 1 of 4
46.3b Cultural Background of the Bible Tape 2 of 4
52.3a Practical Results of the Death of Absolutes Tape 1 of 2
52.3b Practical Results of the Death of Absolutes Tape 2 of 2
53.2a The Modernity of Fundamentalism Tape 1 of 2
53.2b The Modernity of Fundamentalism Tape 2 of 2
53.3 The Christian and Revolution
75.4 Peter versus the Papacy
82.1 Problem of Evil and the God of Love Tape 1 of 2
82.2 Problem of Evil and the God of Love Tape 2 of 2
95.2 Change in Concept of Law in USA Tape 1 of 2
95.3 Change in Concept of Law in USA Tape 2 of 2
95.4 Practical Christian Living
99.1 to 114.2 Biblical Doctrine (63 Tapes)
115.3 Final Choices
128.3 Little People—Little Places
133.1 to 143.3 Revelation (43 Tapes)
144.1 to 153.4 Prophecy (40 Tapes)
157.3 The Christians and Our Moment in History
157.4 The Christian and Government
173.2 The Christian Lawyer under the Scriptures
173.3 A Christian Manifesto

BOOKS

This is a list of books written by Francis Schaeffer. The material you need may well be covered better in one of these books than by the tapes. They are included here as a guide only. The number to the left of a title appears next to corresponding translations of that title throughout.

ENGLISH

1 *Art and the Bible,* IVP (USA)
2 *Ash Heap Lives,* Norfolk
3 *No Little People,* IVP (USA)
4 *Back to Freedom and Dignity,* IVP (USA)
5 *Basic Bible Studies,* Tyndale
6 *The Church at the End of the 20th Century,* IVP (USA)
7 *The Church Before the Watching World,* IVP (USA)
8 *Death in the City,* IVP (USA, UK)
9 *Escape From Reason,* IVP (USA, UK)
10 *Everybody Can Know,* Tyndale SU with Edith Schaeffer
11 *Genesis in Space and Time,* IVP (USA)
12 *The God Who Is There,* IVP, Hodder
13 *He Is There & He Is Not Silent,* Tyndale
14 *How Should We Then Live?,* Revell, Marshall, Morgan & Scott
15 *Joshua and the Flow of Biblical History,* IVP (USA)
16 *Joshua—Study Guide,* IVP (USA)
17 *The Mark of a Christian,* IVP (USA, UK)
18 *The New Super Spirituality,* IVP (USA)
19 *No Final Conflict,* IVP (USA)
20 *Pollution and the Death of Man,* Tyndale
21 *True Spirituality,* Tyndale
22 *Two Contents, Two Realities,* IVP (USA)
23 *Whatever Happened to the Human Race?,* Revell, M,M&S, with C. Everett Koop

RECENT EDITIONS

A Christian Manifesto, Crossway
The Complete Works of Francis A. Schaeffer, Crossway
The Great Evangelical Disaster, Crossway

FOREIGN LANGUAGE EDITIONS: The number to the left of a title will be found against the same title in the English book list.

CHINESE

5 *Basic Bible Studies*
Campus Evangelical Fellowship, Taipei
7 *The Church Before the Watching World*
Christian Chinese Translation Centre
9 *Escape from Reason*
Chinese Christian Literature Council, Hong Kong
17 *The Mark of a Christian*
Christian Witness Press, Hong Kong

CROATIAN

9 *Otkaz Razumu*
Put Zivota

DANISH

13 *Han Har Brudt Verdens Tavshed*
Credo Forlag, Copenhagen
17 *Kaerlighed der Kan Ses*
Lohses Forlag, Fredericia

DUTCH

5 *25 Bijbelstudies*—Buijten & Schipperheijn, Amsterdam
6 *De Kerk Tegen Het Eind Van de 20e EEUW*
8 *De Dood Over de Stad*
11 *Genesis in Riumte en Tijd*
12 *De God Die Leeft*
13 *Hij Es Er, En Hij Spreekt*
17 *Het Kenmerk Van de Christen*
20 *Milieuvervuiling en de Dood Van de Mens*
21 *Leven Door de Geest*

FINNISH

8 *Kuolema Kaupungissa*
Suomennetter Inter-Varsity Pressin, Poukkusilta
9 *Pako Jarjesta*—Sley Kirjat, Joensuu

11 *Kaikki Alkoi Luomisesta*
Suomen Evankelisluterilainen, Ylioppilas
13 *Jumala Ou*
Suomen Evankelisluterilainen, Ylioppilas
17 *Kristityn Tuntomerkki*
Uusi Tie, Helsinki
20 *Kristitty Ja Saastuva Luonto*
Kansan Raamattuseuran Saatio, Helsinki

FRENCH
5 *Les Grands Themes de la Bible*
La Maison de la Bible, Geneva
8 *La Mort Dans le Cite*
La Maison de la Bible, Geneva
9 *Demission de la Raison*
La Maison de la Bible, Geneva
13 *Dieu—Ni Silencieux Ni Lointain*
Editions Trobisch, Kehl
17 *La Marque du Chretien*
Telos, Fontenay-sous-Bois
20 *La Pollution et la Mort de L'Homme*
Ligue pour la Lecture de la Bible, Guebwiller
22 *Impact et Credibilite du Christianisme*
La Maison de la Bible, Geneva

GERMAN
4 *Zuruch zu Freiheit und Wurde*
Hanssler Verlag, Neuhausen-Stuttgart
5 *Die Bibel Zum Thema*
Brockhaus Verlag, Wuppertal; Haus der Bibel, Geneva
6 *Kirche am Ende Des 20 Jahrhunderts*
Brockhaus Verlag, Wuppertal; Haus der Bibel, Geneva
8 *Tod in der Stadt*
Brockhaus Verlag, Wuppertal; Haus der Bibel, Geneva
9 *Preisgabe der Vernunft*
Brockhaus Verlag, Wuppertal; Haus der Bibel, Geneva
11 *Genesis in Raum und Zeit*
Brockhaus Verlag, Wuppertal; Haus der Bibel, Geneva
12 *Gott Ist Keine Illusion*
Brockhaus Verlag, Wuppertal; Haus der Bibel, Geneva

13 . . . *Und er Schweight Nicht*
Brockhaus Verlag, Wuppertal; Haus der Bibel, Geneva
15 *Josua—Gott Will Retten*
Brockhaus Verlag, Wuppertal; Haus der Bibel, Geneva
17 *Das Kennzeichen des Christen*
Brockhaus Verlag, Wuppertal; Haus der Bibel, Geneva
18 *Die Neue Religiose Welle*
Hansser Verlag, Neuhausen-Stuttgart
19 *Der Schopfungsbericht*
Haus der Bibel, Geneva
20 *Das Programmierte Ende*
Brockhaus Verlag, Wuppertal; Haus der Bibel, Geneva
21 *Geistliches Leben—Was Ist Das?*
Brockhaus Verlag, Wuppertal; Haus der Bibel, Geneva
22 *Unsere Welt Soll Sein Wort Horen*
Brockhaus Verlag, Wuppertal; Haus der Bibel, Geneva

HEBREW
12 *The God Who Is There*
Hagefen Publishing, Rishon Le Tsion, Israel
22 *Two Contents, Two Realities*
Hagefen Publishing, Rishon Le Tsion, Israel

HUNGARIAN
8 *Halal A Varosvan*
Evangeliumi Kiado
9 *Menekules ay Ertelemtol*

ICELANDIC
17 *Serkenni Kristins Manns*
Kristilegt Studenta felag, Reykjavik

ITALIAN
6 *La Chiesa Alla Fine del XX Secolo*
Ugo Guanda Editore, Parma
8 *Morte Nelia Citta*
Edizioni Gruppi Biblici Universitari, Rome
9 *Fuga Dalla Ragione*
Edizioni Gruppi Biblici Universitari, Rome

12 *Il Dio Che e La*
Ugo Guanda Editore, Parma
21 *Spiritualita Vera*
Edizioni Voce della Bibbia, Modena

JAPANESE
1 *Art and the Bible*
Kirisutosha Gakusei Kai, issues 631-642, Tokyo
9 *Escape from Reason*
Japan Alliance Mission
12 *The God Who Is There*
Japan Alliance Mission
13 *He Is There and He Is Not Silent*
Japan Alliance Mission
17 *The Mark of a Christian*
Japan Alliance Mission
21 *True Spirituality*
Japan Alliance Mission

KANNADA
5 *Basic Bible Studies*
Scripture Literature Publishers, Bangalore

KOREAN
3 *No Little People*
Word of Life Press, Seoul
5 *Basic Bible Studies*
Word of Life Press, Seoul
6 *The Church at the End of the 20th Century*
Word of Life Press, Seoul
7 *The Church Before the Watching World*
Word of Life Press, Seoul
9 *Escape from Reason*
Word of Life Press, Seoul
11 *Genesis in Space and Time*
Word of Life Press, Seoul
12 *The God Who Is There*
Word of Life Press, Seoul
13 *He Is There and He Is Not Silent*
Word of Life Press, Seoul

17 *Mark of a Christian*
Word of Life Press, Seoul
21 *True Spirituality*
Word of Life Press, Seoul

NORWEGIAN
4 *Frihet og Menneskeverd*
Credo Forlag, Oslo
8 *Jeg Skammer Meg Ikke Ved Evangelict*
Credo Lutherstiftelsen, Oslo
9 *Er Kristendom Forstaelig*
Credo Lutherstiftelsen, Oslo

POLISH
8 *Dokad?*
Powielono Staraniem Prezydium Rady Zjednoczonego
8 *Zycia Chrzescijanskiego; Czyli,* Powielono Staraniem Prezydium Rady Zjednoczonego
9 *Prawdziwego Uduchowienia*
Kosciola Evangelicznego, Warsaw

PORTUGUESE
5 *Os Grandes Temas de Biblia*
Casa da Biblia, Sao Paulo
6 *A Igreja No Ano 2001*
Casa Editora APLIC, Goiania, Goias, Brasil
9 *A Morte da Razao*
Alianca Biblica Universitaria do Brasil, Sao Paulo
17 *O Sinal do Cristao*
Aliance Biblica Universitaria do Brasil, Sao Paulo;
Casa Editora APLIC, Goiania, Boias, Brasil
20 *Poluicao e a Morte do Homem*
Junta de Educacao Religiosa Religiosa e Publicacoes, Rio de Janeiro

RUSSIAN
17 *The Mark of a Christian*
Toronto Christian Mission, Toronto

SPANISH
1 *Arte y Biblia*
Ediciones Evangelicas Europeas, Barcelona
4 *Retorno a la Libertad y la Dignidad*
Ediciones Evangelicas Europeas, Barcelona
5 *25 Estudios Biblicos Basicos*
Ediciones Evangelicas Europeas, Barcelona
6 *La Iglesia al Final del Siglo XX*
Ediciones Evangelicas Europeas, Barcelona
8 *Muerte en la Ciudad*
Ediciones Evangelicas Europeas, Barcelona
9 *Huyendo de la Razon*
Ediciones Evangelicas Europeas, Barcelona
11 *Genesis en el Tiempo y en el Espacio*
Ediciones Evangelicas Europeas, Barcelona
13 *El Esta Presente y No Esta Callado*
Jorge Casas, Barcelona
18 *Los Caminos de la Juventud Hoy*
Ediciones Evangelicas Europeas, Barcelona
20 *Polucion y la Muerte del Hombre*
Casa Bautista de Publicaciones
21 *La Verdadera Espiritualidad*
Pedragosa, Artes graficas, Barcelona

SWEDISH
5 *Grudlaggande Bibelstudier*
Normans Forlag
9 *Pa Flykt Fran Fornuftet*
Ljungbergs Boktryckeri AB, Klippan
12 *Den Gud Som Finns Till*
Interskrift Forlags AB, Herrljunga
17 *Den Kristnes Kannetecken*
Gospel Publications AB, Herrljunga

URDU
17 *The Mark of the Christian*
Masihi Ishaat Khana, Inc., Lahore

FILMS AND VIDEOTAPES

There are film series available in 16mm film and in various videotape formats:

How Should We Then Live?
Whatever Happened to the Human Race?
Reclaiming the World
(Conversations with Francis and Edith Schaeffer)
The Second American Revolution

Both series may be purchased or rented as follows:

USA AND CANADA
To purchase:
FSV Productions
17240 Laurel Road
Los Gatos, CA 95030
Telephone: (408) 356-6677
To rent:
Gospel Films National Film Library
PO Box 455
Muskegon, MICH 49443
Telephone free in USA: 1-800-253-0413
Canada: 616-773-3361

UK AND EIRE
To purchase:
David Payne: Marshall, Morgan & Scott
1 Bath Street
London EC1V9LB
Telephone: 01-251-2925
To rent:
Dave Purnell
British Youth For Christ
52-54 Litchfield Street
Wolverhampton WV1 1DG
Telephone: 0902-771063

or

The Christian World Centre
123 Deansgate
Manchester M60 3BX
Telephone: 061-834-6060

AUSTRALIA, NEW ZEALAND, AND SOUTH AFRICA
To purchase contact David Payne: Marshall, Morgan & Scott as above.

AUSTRALIA
To rent for state and Papua New Guinea branches:
Gospel Film Ministry Ltd.
18-26 Canterbury Road
Heathmont, Victoria 3135
Telephone: 03-729-3777
To rent for non-church viewings (e.g., schools, hospitals, etc.):
Jeff Borg
17 John Street
Tampe 2044
N.S.W.

NEW ZEALAND
To rent:
New Life Pictures
c/o Charles Johnson
McLeavey Road
Ohau RD 20
Levin, New Zealand

SOUTH AMERICA
For distribution, in English, contact Gospel Films National Library as above.

To contact the author, write:

L. G. Parkhurst, Jr.
Christian Life Study Center
P.O. Box 7024
Rochester, Minnesota 55903